SCIENCE & TECHNOLOGY

SOLAR ENERGY

By Wilbur Cross

CHILDRENS PRESS ™

CHICAGO

At Sandia National Laboratories in Albuquerque, New Mexico, 222 heliostats (mirrors) reflect sunlight.

Library of Congress Cataloging in Publication Data

Cross, Wilbur.
  Solar energy.

  (Science and technology)
  Bibliography: p.
  Includes index.
  1. Solar energy. I. Title. II. Series (Chicago, Ill.)
TJ810.C75   1984   333.79′23   83-23243
ISBN 0-516-00511-1

TABLE OF CONTENTS

1. Solar Energy—A Short History .. 5
2. Energy from the Sun . . . 12
3. Harnessing Solar Energy . . . 20
4. Solar Collectors . . . 28
5. Solar Cells and Solar Pioneers .. 38
6. Using Solar Power Today . . . 47
7. Solar Storage Systems and Jobs .. 59
8. Cost of Solar Systems . . . 66
9. Solar Research Projects . . . 76
10. Our Solar Future . . . 87
   Glossary . . . 92
   Bibliography . . . 95
   Index . . . 96
   Picture Acknowledgments . . 100

At the 1882 International Electrical Exposition in the Crystal Palace in London, this demonstration of a 150,000 watt electrical sun amazed spectators. For centuries people have used the power of the sun.

1

Solar Energy — A Short History

AGE-OLD ATTEMPTS TO HARNESS THE SUN

One of the most unusual events in the history of naval battles occurred over two thousand years ago. The Greeks and the Romans were at war. The Roman fleet had sailed into the Sicilian port of Syracuse, where the Greek army was massed to prevent an invasion. The tide of battle seemed to be turning in favor of the Romans, who were preparing to land their forces. But the famous Greek mathematician and inventor Archimedes came up with a brilliant plan.

As the enemy ships approached the shore, Archimedes instructed more than a thousand soldiers to stand along the waterfront and hold their highly polished shields to reflect the sun against the sails of the nearest ships. The concentrated heat from the shields was so intense that the fragile cloth sails began to smolder. As fires broke out on the sails, the Roman captains hastily retreated, giving the Greeks time to strengthen their ranks and prevent an invasion.

This dramatic episode was one of the first, and certainly one of the most graphic, examples of using sun power—or as we commonly refer to it today, *solar energy*.

THE FIRST SOLAR HOMES

Solar heating goes back so far in history that no one really knows when and where man first used it deliberately to make life more comfortable. Some of the earliest and most efficient solar homes were those used by dwellers in the desert regions of Egypt, Libya, and Algeria. In those barren areas of North Africa, the sun beats down with a fierce heat during the day. Yet at night, temperatures can be fifty or sixty degrees cooler. The builders of simple homes near scattered desert oases learned a useful fact thousands of years ago: If they constructed their houses with thick walls of mud and sand, the heat was absorbed by those materials during the day so the interiors stayed as cool as caves. At night, the walls retained much of the heat they had absorbed and kept the interiors from becoming chilly.

These same tribes also learned and passed down to succeeding generations primitive methods of using the sun to dry and preserve foods, bake bread, bleach cloth, and harden mud into bricks that were surprisingly enduring and strong. At some point in history, several peoples—notably the ancient Egyptians—learned how to use the sun to help preserve the dead as mummies. It was no wonder that eventually the sun itself was considered one of the most important gods in the Egyptian religion.

SOLAR HEATING IN EARLY AMERICA

By strange coincidence, primitive Indians who lived in what is now the southwestern part of the United States discovered some of the same solar secrets as the Egyptians. They constructed adobe dwellings with very thick clay walls and were thus able to "capture" the heat of the sun to keep them warm during cold nights. Tribes in some locations, such as those who inhabited the cliff dwellings of Mesa Verde in southwestern Colorado, purposely selected southern exposures so that even in the winter season, when the sun was lower in the sky than at other times of the year, the walls absorbed the sun's radiation in a very effective way.

In the more northerly climates of America, the sun was not respected as much as in the south. Still the Indians used the power of the sun whenever they could.

Years later when the pioneers settled in North America they also took advantage of solar power when they could. For example, many

These two examples of early solar heating systems, Balcony House ruins (left) and Spruce Tree House (right), are found in Mesa Verde National Park in Cortez, Colorado. The Indians built homes that took full advantage of the materials they had available to them. The Pueblo Indians and Cliff Dwellers used adobe (sun-dried bricks). The Indians in the Andes Mountains of South America and Indians in Mexico also used adobe for construction.

of the oldest homes in the Northeast not only face south, but make use of surrounding areas of slate and flat rocks, which retain heat long after the sun has set.

Many early greenhouses in northern climes protected delicate plants during cold nights by using bases of slate, brick, and rock to keep interiors warm for many hours with no other heat than that produced by solar rays.

ORIGIN AND NATURE OF EARLY SOLAR INVENTIONS

In the history of solar energy there is a long and puzzling gap between primitive devices to harness the sun and those of more recent times. Did man forget that the sun could be an able servant? Or did other forms of energy, such as peat and coal and eventually petroleum, prove to be more efficient for conventional heating and cooking?

Both of these reasons are valid. But some historians believe that the sun lost out as populations shifted and new cultures replaced old ones in the world struggle for power. When Egypt and Greece and other nations in the sun-flooded Mediterranean region waned in power and the nations of central and northern Europe came into prominence, the dominant peoples lived in regions that were colder and rainier. Harnessing the sun in foggy old London, for instance, was hardly as easy as doing so in ancient, sun-drenched Thebes.

In the seventeenth century, scientists in Europe began "rediscovering" the sun. An optician in France, knowledgeable in the use of lenses and magnifying glasses, undertook some remarkably practical experiments. He proved that the rays of the sun, focused and concentrated through glass prisms, could melt copper and fuse pieces of iron. In the 1690s, an Italian scientist invented a solar furnace that was even hotter and in one instance was able to shatter one of the hardest substances on earth, a diamond.

The most successful solar furnace of that era was perfected by a French scientist, Antoine Lavoisier, using a concave lens some four feet in diameter. By focusing sunlight on an area the size of a pinhead, he managed to produce heat in excess of 3,000 degrees Fahrenheit. That is intense enough to melt most of the metals of his day, including platinum, which is very difficult to fuse. The year was 1774, an important date in the history of energy. Lavoisier used his invention to demonstrate that heat itself was not an element and that substances did not lose weight in the process of being melted.

TRANSFERRING HEAT INTO MECHANICAL POWER

The concept of harnessing the rays of the sun to power an engine apparently did not occur to engineers until the middle of the nineteenth century, when a number of experimental models were designed. The first one of any significance was built in 1870 by a Swedish inventor, John Ericsson. He was best known as the designer of the *Monitor,* the ironclad Civil War gunboat used by the Union navy in the historic battle against the Confederate *Merrimac.*

Ericsson's invention used an enormous mirror, some sixteen feet long, to generate steam. The steam then powered a single-cylinder engine. Discouraged by a lack of interest in an engine that could run only when the sun was shining, Ericsson converted his engine to coal

This lens was constructed for the French Academy in the eighteenth century. Antoine Lavoisier, one of the scientists who worked on this project, later built a solar furnace that was capable of reaching temperatures of more than 3,000 degrees Fahrenheit.

and sold tens of thousands to interested buyers. Solar power seemed as far removed from the practical world as the sun itself.

Much more practical was an engine built by another inventor, A.G. Eneas, thirty-one years later. Set to work pumping water, it was successfully installed in a desert area near Phoenix, Arizona, where there was hardly ever a cloud in the sky. A local newspaper, the *Arizona Republican,* expressed amazement that so much work could be accomplished without any fuel being consumed.

"The reflector," explained the 1901 account, "somewhat resembles a huge umbrella, open and inverted at such an angle as to receive the full effect of the sun's rays on 1,788 little mirrors lining its inside surface." The device also had a boiler, where steam was generated, and a pipe that carried the steam to a nearby engine house.

The whole thing worked quite efficiently. But the reflector was so delicate—more than thirty-three feet in diameter—that it was demolished by a sudden windstorm and the Arizona solar project was abandoned. Another solar pump, with a fifty-horsepower engine, was built ten years later in Egypt and used for irrigating fields along the Nile River near the city of Meadi.

COULD THE SUN PRODUCE ELECTRICITY?

This was a challenging question around the beginning of the twentieth century. It was particularly intriguing to scientists and inventors because electricity could be *stored* and would thus overcome the major problem of most solar inventions: that their practical usage was limited to the hours when the sun was actually shining.

Most of the inventions failed, with one notable exception. Frank Shuman, an engineer in Tacony, Pennsylvania, built an experimental plant to capture the sun. He used glass-covered troughs filled with a few inches of water. Because they were painted black, they became very hot, causing the water to circulate and supply power to an electrical generator.

Shuman's demonstrations were so convincing that he was able to attract financial backers and build the Eastern Sun Power Company, the world's first solar electric power plant. Not surprisingly, it was also located in Egypt, land of perpetual sun. But it was an ungainly plant, requiring a sun-collecting area of almost fourteen thousand square feet and troughs more than two hundred feet long. The amount of electricity produced was far less than had been estimated. Ironically, the Eastern Sun Power Company, using "free fuel," went out of business because it was cheaper in the long run, and much more practical, to generate electricity by burning coal or fuel oil.

DEVELOPMENTS LAGGING IN THE UNITED STATES

Until the middle of the twentieth century, most of the history of solar energy covers activities in countries other than the United States. Research and development were much more advanced abroad, not only in Egypt, but also in Australia, South Africa, France, U.S.S.R., Japan, and Israel. There just was not enough incentive in America, where fossil fuels such as coal and petroleum were in abundant supply and still quite cheap.

The only American product with any range of acceptance was the solar water heater, which was popular in Florida as early as the 1920s,

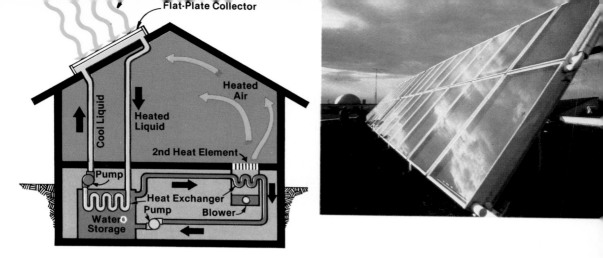

Flat-Plate Collector

Heated Air

Cool Liquid

Heated Liquid

2nd Heat Element

Pump

Heat Exchanger

Pump

Blower

Water Storage

The liquid heating in the collectors (above) flows to a storage tank. A heat exchanger is used to transfer the heat to water in the tank. Then the cooled liquid is returned to the collectors to be reheated. The hot water in the tank is pumped to another heat exchanger, which heats the air blown into the house.

These single-glazed flat plate collectors (right) supply solar-heated water at the Bronx High School of Science.

and later in California and the Southwest. The depression at the start of the 1930s motivated sales of just about any device that would save money and even generated a short-lived flurry of interest in other solar inventions.

One of the most significant events in the modern history of solar-heating development occurred in 1939. That year, a group at the Massachusetts Institute of Technology (M.I.T.) constructed a small house near Boston with a rooftop solar collector. Water heated by the sun circulated through copper pipes covered with three layers of glass. When the water reached a high temperature, it flowed to the cellar to a huge, well-insulated storage tank. Air ducts then absorbed heat from the water and circulated it to the rest of the house through a blower system.

This house was the prototype of other, much more efficient, solar homes that would be built in the 1980s. Yet it was scrapped after almost twenty years of experimentation as being far too expensive to design and build for most home owners.

The history of solar power has always been cursed by an ironic truth: Although sunshine is free, the means of collecting and using it are more expensive than almost any other form of energy available.

Energy From The Sun

HOW ENERGY COMES FROM THE SUN

Solar energy is basically very simple: heat and light coming from the sun. But many problems and complications, both direct and indirect, arise when man tries to use that natural heat and light for a variety of purposes.

There is no doubt that the solar source is boundless. Scientists estimate, for example, that the sunlight that falls on the surface of our globe every twenty-four hours is enough to satisfy all of the energy needs of all the nations of the world for the next fifteen years. Phrased another way, the sunlight that bathes the earth over a period of just two weeks is equivalent in energy to *all* of the oil and natural gas and coal and other fuels that exist on, or under, the earth.

Yet today we are content to try to harness only the tiniest fraction of all that energy. Why? Mainly because we cannot use any of this energy in a practical way until scientists and engineers and inventors can perfect equipment for collecting, converting, storing, and transmitting it efficiently. People are not willing to use solar energy in any form until the cost is less than—or at least comparable to—the cost of oil, gas, coal, or other conventional fuels.

There are some important exceptions to this viewpoint, as will be discussed later. An obvious one is the use of solar energy for space vehicles, where fuel storage space is limited and critical.

THE SUN AS THE SOURCE OF ALL ENERGY ON EARTH

It may sound like a contradiction, but the sun actually is the source, whether directly or indirectly, of *all* energy stored on our planet. What about oil and coal and gas? These fuels and others were formed millions of years ago when the sun generated chemical and mechanical reactions that transformed various organic substances into the materials we know and use.

All forms of life depend upon the sun and its rays. Even in the perpetually dark depths of the sea, the ocean currents and chemical changes that sustain marine life are set in motion by the sun. When the sun evaporates water—whether from oceans, lakes, rivers, or ponds—it forms clouds and controls the cycles of drought and rain everywhere on earth. We use the word *atmosphere* in regard to climate and weather. The atmosphere is actually a thin layer that encircles the globe and protects us from certain rays that would be harmful if they were not blocked and scattered into outer space. The atmosphere is controlled by the sun and actually permits beneficial rays to filter through to the earth where they are vital in sustaining all plant and animal life. We hardly realize that energy is the end result, making it possible for seeds to sprout, for plants to grow, and for animals and humans to thrive and develop.

Another word that we hear more and more often today is *radiation*. This refers to rays generated by the sun that reach us in many forms, including infrared, ultraviolet, and what we regard as ordinary sunlight. Though all carry endless amounts of energy, and though the heat of the sun may sometimes seem overpowering on a hot summer day, the energy is scattered and diffuse. From the standpoint of practical application, this means that solar energy has to be collected over a wide area, concentrated, and stored in order to be used for energy purposes.

Scientists refer to solar energy as the electromagnetic radiation produced on the sun and radiated over some 93 million miles at a speed of 186,000 miles per second. When sunlight reaches the earth's air space, it provides energy at a surprisingly constant rate: about 430 Btus per hour for every square foot of area. A Btu (British thermal unit) is the common measure of all forms of energy—the amount of heat required to raise the temperature of one pound of water one degree Fahrenheit.

When sunlight reaches the earth, it theoretically supplies 130 watts in terms of electrical power units for each square foot during a one-hour period. But taking into account the hours of darkness, cloud cover, and absorption by the atmosphere, the actual amount of energy is equal to little more than fifteen watts. And when even the most efficient solar systems go to work, the ultimate energy output is likely to be little more than two or three watts! Obviously there is an enormous challenge when it comes to collecting, storing, and using energy from the sun.

THE NATURE OF THIS GREAT FURNACE, THE SUN

The sun is about *one million times* the size of the earth. Gigantic nuclear explosions are constantly taking place within its interior. During these reactions, temperatures reach more than 25 million degrees Fahrenheit, converting atoms from one form into another. Fortunately for mankind, much of this heat is radiated in directions away from the earth, preventing us all from being scorched to death.

The world's largest vertical axis wind turbine (left) is located on Magdalen Island in the Gulf of St. Lawrence, Canada. It produces 250 kilowatts in a 35-kilometer-an-hour wind. Close-up of a solar eruption.

It has been estimated that the earth receives only the tiniest fraction of the sun's radiation—about two billionths in all.

The words *energy* and *power* are often used interchangeably, especially in discussions about solar power or solar energy. Actually, there is an important distinction to bear in mind. Think of it this way: The sun produces *energy*, great quantities of it, as has been described. What reaches the earth in the form of radiation is energy, not solar power.

Power is the rate at which the energy is produced. For example, a *kilowatt* (one thousand watts) is the unit commonly used to measure power. To measure solar energy, we use the term *kilowatt hour*, that is, the energy expended by one kilowatt in one hour.

Power can come from sources not normally associated with the sun. A good example is hydroelectric power: The force of water running downhill turns machinery to generate the electric power used in homes and industry. Why should this be classed as solar in origin? Because sea water, evaporated by the sun, rises into the air, falls on high ground, and supplies the rivers and streams that are harnessed for the generation of electricity.

Strange as it may seem, windmills that pump water or generate electricity also derive their power from the sun. Their giant blades spin because of the wind. And the wind in turn occurs because the sun has heated the air in varying degrees and thus has created air currents.

We might even go so far as to say that the growth of plants is powered by the sun, whether the plants are tiny one-celled plankton floating in the sea or many-limbed giants growing in mountain forests. What actually happens is that sunlight is converted into chemical energy through the manufacture of carbohydrates. The process is known scientifically as photosynthesis.

These are but a few of the ways in which solar energy becomes solar power.

SOLAR ENERGY—EVEN AN ELEMENT IN MAN'S CULTURE

A solar scientist recently stated that "solar energy is a field for visionary inventors and entrepreneurs." He likened the methods and inventions of the 1980s as being no more advanced today than the Model T was when the automobile was becoming popular in America.

As engineers and inventors have pointed out, it will be many years before solar energy devices will really be efficient and economical for a wide variety of purposes. Present solar power systems involve great amounts of waste, which tend to make them expensive.

We think of the United States as being very advanced in most fields of technology. Yet America lags behind a number of other countries that have been putting solar energy to use during the past few decades. Australia, France, Israel, and South Africa have been perfecting methods and producing equipment at a much higher rate.

Since the middle of this century, the Soviet Union is said to have placed high priority on methods and devices for harnessing the sun. One objective has been to use solar energy for a wide range of civilian requirements, thus freeing other forms of energy (such as coal and oil) for military. and industrial uses. Tashkent, a city of a million people on the Syr Darya River in central Asia, has for many years been the site of one of the world's greatest solar research programs. Through the knowledge and expertise gained there, the Soviets expect to establish plants in many locations for the generation of massive amounts of electricity, thereby vastly reducing reliance on conventional fossil fuels. Smaller systems are also being devised for use in

isolated regions, for special types of projects, and for the ongoing space program.

In Israel and Australia it is quite easy to buy solar water heaters. In the United States, though, they are hard to find, and very expensive at that. In Japan, it is not uncommon for schools to have heat and hot water supplied almost entirely by the sun. Japan is also a leader in the production of solar cells (which will be discussed in a later chapter). Today, that country's industries and government are spending many billions of dollars on a twenty-five-year program known as "The Sunshine Project."

"In Israel," says a scientist who has been working on numerous projects in Tel Aviv, "the sun is part of our culture. By that, I don't mean that we do a lot of sunbathing, but that we have to depend on our natural resources for our existence. And the sun is without doubt the greatest of all resources."

When modern Israel came into being, the sun was widely used for low-cost energy systems since it was all but impossible to develop other forms of energy quickly and effectively. Increasing turmoil in the Middle East and the problems of obtaining enough oil and gas served to boost Israel's reliance on the sun as a source of power.

Why haven't some of the developing nations looked to Israel as an example and begun perfecting methods of tapping the sun for vital energy needs? Something in their culture is missing, over and beyond

Instruments to measure radiation from the sun (left), improved solar panels for residential units (middle), and development of improved heat-producing materials for solar panels have been by-products of America's space program.

the lack of qualified technologists. They continue to use the sun only for the age-old purposes, such as drying and preserving foods, bleaching cloth, and growing crops.

Until recently, America also was not yet ready to accept the sun as an ally. But that situation will change with increasing rapidity as techniques are explored and benefits realized.

THE SEARCH FOR BENEFITS FROM THE SUN

Much of the focus on solar energy in the United States came about as a result of the space program. When it was realized that spacecraft would have to function without conventional batteries or fuels, solar power became the obvious alternative. This led to the development of the solar cell, first workable in space in the mid-1950s.

Dramatic though the projects were, their costs were prohibitive. Yet there are many possible benefits to be derived through less expensive and exotic applications. Here are a few of the kinds of projects and equipment we can expect to see in widespread use in many parts of the United States.

Turbines. The method for generating electricity on a large scale is referred to as "solar-thermal conversion." Research has been conducted by such well-known organizations as Westinghouse, Honey-well, and Aerospace Corporation, and by the University of Arizona. A number of public utilities have also committed research funds to methods for using the sun's energy to generate electric power.

Water heaters. These will be mass-produced as gas and electric hot-water heaters are now. However, the most beneficial and effective types will continue to be those built into a home's utility system at the time of construction or modernization.

Evaporators. Used mainly by industry, evaporators make use of the sun to separate certain elements from liquids. One of the most common examples is extracting salt from sea water by evaporation.

Navigational aids. Solar-powered batteries have been used increasingly in remote areas that are serviced infrequently because of great difficulty. They power such equipment as unmanned lighthouses, aircraft beacons, and emergency communications equipment.

Stills. Though largely experimental, solar stills may be one answer to the growing problem of supplying populations with fresh water. One still has a collector that is twelve thousand square feet in size and can produce more than five thousand gallons of fresh water from salt water every twenty-four hours. Solar stills have been in operation for generations, many of them on islands in the Mediterranean where rainfall is negligible.

Stoves. Solar cookers are available for campers optimistic enough to expect the sun to be shining at the sites selected. But commercial cooking equipment may not be too far in the future, enabling bakeries and food processors to cut their fuel costs tremendously by calling on the sun for help.

Kilns. The lumber industry has recently had its eye on kilns that will hasten the drying-out steps in processing certain types of lumber. These utilize air heaters that collect their heat from the sun.

Heat storage units. The most challenging of all of the potential benefits from the sun relates to methods and equipment for storing sun-generated heat during long periods of darkness or inclement weather. Progress is slow (as will be described in a later chapter), but the end results seem assured.

3

HARNESSING SOLAR ENERGY

GEOGRAPHY'S INFLUENCE ON SOLAR ENERGY

Insolation is, by definition, the rate at which solar energy is delivered to any given unit of a surface. *Solar insolation* was established by Samuel Langley, an American astronomer, as a way of indicating how much sun was striking an area over a period of time. In recognition of his work, the "langley" has been adopted as a unit for calculating the sun's effect.

For a long time—since Langley's work in the late nineteenth century—his unit of measurement was important only to scientists engaged in research. Now, however, it has assumed great significance worldwide as a means of geographical comparison. It serves to answer questions like these:

In what regions of the world is sunlight the strongest and most consistent?

How much more effective would a solar water heater be in the Southwest than in New England?

What are the best months for operating solar devices in northern Florida?

Which sales territories in the United States would be most promising for a company about to market a new solar device?

What is the difference between summer and winter in measuring solar energy in a given location?

On the average, what are the differences in solar strength in a given location, mornings versus afternoons?

It is natural to assume that geography plays a very important role in determining the practicality of developing solar energy systems around the globe. We might guess that sunlight would be much stronger over the Sahara than over central Florida. But the question is: *How much* stronger?

As meteorological equipment becomes more reliable and the weather experts more consistent in their evaluations, solar scientists are better able to make decisions and solve problems. They have determined that the sun, which obviously is hottest across the United States in the summer, will range from five hundred to seven hundred langleys on an average summer day. In the winter, however, the average will drop to less than three hundred langleys and perhaps to as low as one hundred.

Weather conditions are important in any consideration of solar energy. The fact that one location is considerably hotter than another on a year-round basis does not necessarily mean that it is more desirable for the development of solar power. *Reliability* is another key factor. A location with extremely variable and often unpredictable weather may be unattractive for solar installations. Unfortunately, when we think of energy and power, we think of situations in which a switch can be flicked ''on'' or ''off'' at will. Until energy storage devices are much improved, solar must be considered the least reliable of all energy sources.

Ironically, the sun itself is the main culprit when it comes to changes in weather. The sun directly affects the way water is evaporated and clouds are formed. Where cloud covers are thick, most solar energy simply bounces right back up into space. It has been demonstrated that more than one third of all the solar energy that reaches the earth's atmosphere is lost in this manner. Another 20 percent bounces around in the atmosphere, doing little more than warming the clouds and high strata of air.

In one way, the sun does recompense mankind for its frivolity in the matter of cloud formation. Since the sun's radiation is considerably stronger at the equator than at the North or South Poles, there is a constant churning in the atmosphere. Tropical air rises when

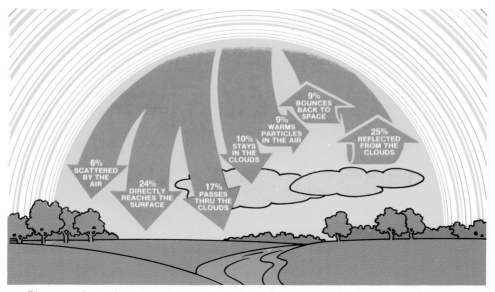

Diagram shows how the atmosphere affects the amount of solar energy that reaches the earth. Percentages are approximate.

heated by the sun, while cool polar air is sucked away from the Arctic and Antarctic regions to replace it. The result is a continual series of air currents circulating around the earth. These currents are further strengthened and diverted so that we enjoy the phenomenon of *wind,* varying from gentle breezes to violent gales. So, a certain percentage of the energy lost in cloud cover is regained when windmills are used to harness the movements of air.

Wind power, according to a United States government booklet, is a good example of "the *indirect* conversion of solar energy." It occurs most often on farms where mills are used to pump water and sometimes to turn wind generators that produce electricity for local use. Some of today's experimental generators have enormous blades and can produce enough electricity to supply whole communities with power.

In addition, much more energy is recaptured by harnessing the rushing rivers and streams that have been strengthened by the sun's creation of clouds.

Meteorologists and solar experts have pooled their knowledge and experience to chart the average annual hours of sunshine in regions across the United States. A solar map shows quite distinctly and graphically where solar energy has a promising future. California,

Arizona, New Mexico, and parts of Texas are on the high side. The central United States, from the Canadian border south all the way to the Gulf of Mexico, is surprisingly low, regardless of the latitude. And the East Coast is spotty, varying from quite high to very low.

THE SUN AND OUTER SPACE

There is one place with a never-ending supply of sunshine, no matter what the season, month, or time of day: *outer space.* Solar energy in the regions beyond the earth's atmosphere is not only continual, but undiluted and intense.

When scientists first made plans for putting satellites into orbit in the 1950s, they had in mind powering equipment aboard the spacecraft almost exclusively with sophisticated batteries and electronic energy systems. Some of these had been used successfully on battlefields and in the air during World War II.

As spacecraft became more and more complex, plans were proposed for probing farther into outer space. It was soon evident that conventional power sources would not suffice. What these projects called for were power supplies that could not be used up, even though future missions might take many months and even years.

Solar energy was the only solution to the power problem.

In 1958, the *Vanguard I* satellite was sent into orbit around the earth. It was the first American spacecraft to rely on solar cells to generate electricity from sunlight. By later standards, *Vanguard I* was limited in design and capabilities. But the solar cells powering a radio transmitter performed so well that broadcasts from outer space continued for many years after the launching.

By the late 1970s, several thousand satellites using the sun as the basic source of power had been put into orbit. One reason why they have performed so well is that the power requirements are low. There is no great electrical drain on the system at any one time—nothing like what is required when an electric range or air conditioner is turned on at home and suddenly requires heavy wattage. What happens in space is that the solar cells (of which there may be many thousands on a single spacecraft) convert the sunlight that strikes them into electric current. The current charges other sets of cells, which in turn provide power for all the circuits.

Skylab, America's first manned space station, was equipped with what was at the time the most complex solar power system ever launched into outer space. It was the forerunner of spaceships with energy wings, fragile panels that unfolded and projected from the ships once they reached orbit. *Skylab,* a midget in comparison with later space stations, mounted a pair of wings, each 28 feet by 30 feet, containing about 1,150 feet of solar surfacing.

The wings converted sunlight into electric power that operated laboratory equipment inside the ship. In full sunlight the wings produced more than twelve thousand watts, functioning steadily at fifty-five volts.

SOLAR PROBLEMS AND SOLUTIONS

Scientists and engineers of the National Aeronautics and Space Administration (NASA) had to overcome a number of difficult problems in order to make use of the sun for powering space vehicles. Among them:

• Solar power is very expensive, especially in a system as demand-

Skylab was the first manned spaceship that relied almost entirely on solar energy for its power. Even when one of the solar wings was damaged and had to be repaired and adjusted in space, the crew had enough power to complete the scientific experiments that had been planned for Skylab.

ing and sensitive as a spacecraft. Everything must be designed to function precisely, with one or more backup systems to protect the primary one in the event of any kind of failure.

• Outer space is not, as many people think, a void filled with absolutely nothing except planets millions of miles apart and the satellites man has placed in orbit. Tiny particles and specks of dust are becoming more common after the thousands of launchings that have taken place. Colliding with the speed of a bullet, they can damage delicate solar wings and cells upon impact.

• Solar cells are weakened when exposed to the heat of the sun, which is twice as bright in outer space as at the earth's surface. Enormous drops in temperature occur when a spacecraft is in the shadow of the earth, even for very brief spells. The sudden impact of the sun when a craft leaves the region of darkness affects solar equipment adversely.

• Solar cells and panels must face the sun directly in order to function effectively. Since a spaceship is constantly changing position, intricate mechanisms have to be designed to control the solar surfaces continuously.

A space solar power system designed to support an industry based on asteroid retrieval. Asteroids contain major elements that could be put to industrial use. The solar power station in the foreground would provide electronic power for the settlement in the background.

Farsighted scientists have envisioned enormous, earth-orbiting space stations powered entirely by solar energy capable of sustaining their needs for decades on end. They have also already conceived plans for solar power stations. These would generate electricity by using one of several workable methods, including solar cells, or vast arrays of mirrors. Such power stations would be as much as ten miles in length and cost as much as $30 billion. They could, however, generate billions of watts of electricity.

The electricity would be converted into microwaves at the space station, orbiting some 23,000 miles above the earth, and beamed to ground-based receiving stations with huge antennas. In principle, it would be much like beaming waves from a radar transmitter to an antenna.

The cost of this kind of solar energy would be higher than nuclear energy at first, because of the expense of constructing the equipment. But the power would be totally reliable, no matter what the season or weather conditions, and would be available to even the remotest locations on the face of the earth.

THE SUN AND THE SEA

A French scientist named Jacques d'Arsonval, while studying the oceans in the 1870s, made the astonishing prophecy that whole populations could be heated by capturing warmth from the sea. His concept was actually quite complex, based on the fact that there are substantial temperature differences between the waters in the ocean depths and those on the surface. In tropical regions, the differences can be great, ranging from the low 80s on the surface to less than 40 degrees Fahrenheit at depths of two thousand feet.

This theory was later to be referred to as Ocean Thermal Energy Conversion, or OTEC. Picture a power plant floating in the warm waters off the coast of southern Florida. It might look like any other power plant, designed around a large generator for producing electricity. Instead of being run by steam from burning coal or oil, however, the generator would be turned by vapor.

Where would the vapor come from? Instead of using water heated into steam, the ocean power plant would use ammonia. Ammonia can be vaporized easily by heating it with warm water from the surface of the ocean, say at a temperature of 80 degrees Fahrenheit. The ammonia would then be condensed into a liquid by cool water from the depths, at a temperature of 50 degrees or less.

As ammonia runs through a cycle from liquid to vapor, it expands into a gas. The force of this expanding gas can then be used to turn a generator, thus producing electricity without ever requiring the consumption of fuel. The efficiency range of this form of solar power is very low, particularly since some of the electricity produced by the generator must be used to pump cold water from the ocean depths to the surface plant. Nevertheless, the costs are also negligible and the equipment functions on natural forces that are always at work, as reliable as the tides themselves.

One forecast claimed that OTEC generating plants, positioned strategically along the Gulf Stream alone, could produce enough electricity to supply the entire United States.

SOLAR COLLECTORS

THE CHALLENGE OF SOLAR POWER

Given all of the problems we have had in recent years with oil embargoes, air pollution from burning coal, and the defects in nuclear reactors, why hasn't solar energy been developed far beyond the present stage?

The question is natural. Solar power would come from a boundless and totally reliable source. It would eliminate water and air pollution caused by the consumption of fossil fuels. It would be available to people in the remotest regions of the world. It would prevent the depletion of limited energy resources.

The answer to the question is not so simple. Almost every scientist, engineer, or specialist working in this field sooner or later describes solar power as "challenging." That is, it taxes the knowledge and insight and experience of those who experiment with solar energy to solve two basic problems:

(1) Despite the abundance of solar energy, it is much more *diffuse* than most of us realize, even during a baking hot summer afternoon. To produce electricity, or just to heat a large home, requires collectors with very large surface areas. Collectors are costly to install and to maintain. Many must be individually designed to take full advantage of the site and the region, and at best are likely to be low in efficiency. Furthermore, the diffuseness varies at any given location from one season to another, and often from day to day.

(2) Sunshine is *intermittent*. Even the very best of sunlit sites is

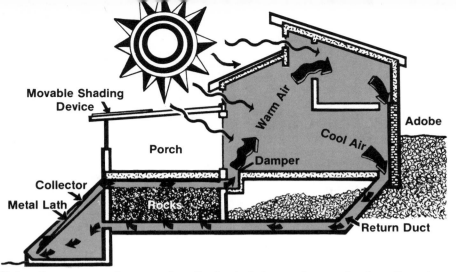

Follow the arrows and you see how the heated air or water can rise from the solar collector and move through the solar system.

limited in the number of hours that can be counted on during an average day. Unexpected shifts in the weather can turn out to be more than simply an inconvenience, leaving a home or other facility dependent upon other sources of power.

In both of the cases above, the best—if not *only*—solution is to design and install systems that will store electricity or heat, or both, during the interim. In many cases, such storage facilities would have to be bulky, unsightly, and certainly expensive. They might consist of batteries that are charged by solar power when the sun is strong, hot water tanks, or heat-retaining solids, such as brick, slate, or stone.

THE TASK OF COLLECTING SUNBEAMS

If you have ever held a magnifying glass to focus rays of sun on a piece of paper until it smolders and burns, you already know one of the problems of putting solar energy to work. You have to tilt the glass in just such a way that the rays come into strong focus—otherwise, nothing happens. That is true of any solar collector, whether it is a flat sheet, a solar cell, a magnifying glass, or a parabolic mirror. Its effectiveness is weakened, or entirely lost, if the angle is not correct.

The sun plays games with everyone who tries to set up a permanent type of collector. The sun is constantly changing position. The earth

29

complicates matters by varying in the way its spins on its axis, not only during changes in seasons but on a much more frequent basis.

Engineers who design equipment to capture the sun's energy know that they can generate a great amount of heat if the rays of sun are concentrated by a collector at a single point. A concave (curving inward) mirror is so excellent a collector that it is used in the design of an interesting consumer product—a solar cooker. Such a cooker can be made by using a number of small mirrors to form a kind of bowl. Reflected to a pan, the sun's rays make it hot enough to cook food or boil liquids.

This rather simple method was used in the nineteenth century, and even hundreds of years before that, for a number of practical purposes. Inventors claimed to have harnessed the sun to run printing presses, power vehicles and boats, pump water, and perform many other common tasks. In effect what they were doing was boiling water to make steam, which in turn operated the machinery in question. Few of these inventions were efficient, and even fewer had any commercial potential.

The biggest challenge is one of *degree,* literally. A collector made of flat plates or tubes, such as the kind designed for the partial heating of hot water and the interior of homes, is limited. It will heat water to a temperature of about 200 degrees Fahrenheit on a clear, sunny day. But that is hardly enough to produce the large quantities of steam necessary to perform a major task such as generating electricity.

One solution, says a government handbook, is the use of *concentrating collectors*. "These devices gather the solar energy falling on a larger surface and direct it onto a smaller one. The ratio between the two areas is the degree of concentration. The higher the concentration, the higher the temperature and the greater the efficiency."

Such collectors employ a method called "tracking." That is, they literally track, or follow, the sun as it changes position in the heavens. Of course, this procedure calls for complicated and costly equipment. More and more collectors are being guided by computers, since few human beings are talented enough (or patient enough) to spend long hours tracking the sun.

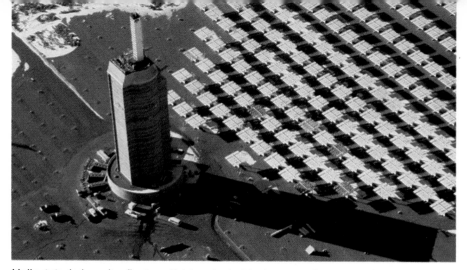

Heliostats (mirrors) reflect sunlight on test object mounted on a 200-foot-tall tower at Sandia National Laboratories.

One example is known as a *heliostat,* made of mirrored surfaces and operated by clockwork so that the sun is constantly reflected in one direction. One type looks like a series of venetian blinds that have been silvered and mounted on a turntable. Their searing beams are focused on a boiler at the top of a high tower. A "forest" of heliostats, covering more than one square mile and each producing temperatures of more than 1,000 degrees Fahrenheit, could produce enough power for a town of some 35,000 homes. But these heliostats could do so only if the sunlight were constant enough and strong enough over a period of a year to provide the power expected.

THE SEARCH FOR COMPATIBLE MATERIALS

The most common solar collectors are the *flat plate* collector and the *parabolic* collector. The former usually is a combination of coils of tubing arranged on a metal plate with panes of glass. These are set in a frame so that one of the flat sides faces the sun. In order to absorb more of the heat rays, the overall plate is painted black. Insulation is set between the collector plate and the rooftop or other foundation on which the unit rests. The insulation prevents heat loss between the collecting point and the area where the heat is being directed.

Thomason solar house in District Heights, Washington, D.C.

Very simple collectors can be made of corrugated metal, although others may be honeycombs of copper tubing, plastic sheeting, plastic pipe, or a variety of other substances. Most use running water to carry the heat from the collector to the unit being heated. Aluminum and brass tubing and plating are also used on some collectors. Where the objective is a limited amount of heating (such as warming a swimming pool), black plastic may suffice.

Solar collectors for individual projects need not always be complicated or expensive. One home builder, for example, made an effective collector out of corrugated aluminum roofing that is commonly sold for barn roofs. He painted it black and covered it with a single layer of clear glass. A plastic pipe along the top of the collector was punched with holes so that water would flow down the corrugated valleys into a gutter and then into a two-thousand-gallon storage tank in the basement. The water tank was surrounded by stones. As these stones became heated, a blower transferred the heat from them to conduits leading to various parts of the house.

Some systems use the flow of hot water itself for heating, running pipes down the interiors of wall spaces. The water, in either case, is eventually pumped back up to the roof where it continues its heating cycle. Electronic devices, sensitive to light, turn the water pump off at night or when the sky is too cloudy to heat the roof collector.

Parabolic dish solar collectors

Such solar heating installation, of course, will function only when there is a reasonably steady flow of sunshine over all seasons. Almost invariably, a backup heating system is needed, using conventional fuels such as oil, natural gas, or electricity.

Parabolic collectors are used more often with large commercial solar energy projects and in any situation where higher temperatures (over 200 degrees Fahrenheit) are required. These are of the type discussed earlier, resembling bowls, that concentrate the sun's rays on a certain point. Some parabolic collectors are made up of a single mirrored surface, although others consist of many separate elements positioned to form a bowl or arc. One variation uses a series of horizontal tubes filled with water. The tubes are positioned so as to form a curving trough rather than a flat surface.

The advantage of this kind of arrangement is twofold. First, the tubes tend to intensify the heat by interacting as the flowing water heats up in each one. Second, the curve catches the intensity of the sun as it changes position more effectively than do flat plates.

Engineers and inventors are continually coming up with ingenious new ideas for capturing the sun's energy. An experimental house built by architects and engineers at California State Polytechnic College is an interesting example. Called *Sky-Therm,* it was built with a roof covered with clear plastic bags filled with water—not unlike a series

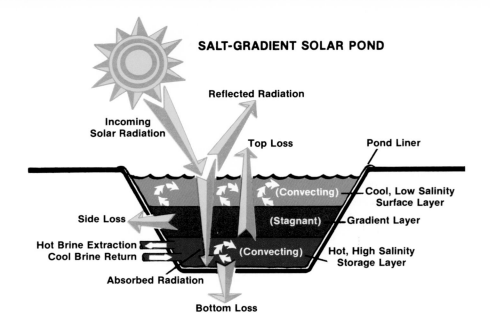

SALT-GRADIENT SOLAR POND

Reflected Radiation

Incoming
Solar Radiation

Top Loss

Pond Liner

(Convecting) — Cool, Low Salinity
Surface Layer

Side Loss

(Stagnant) — Gradient Layer

Hot Brine Extraction
Cool Brine Return

(Convecting)

Hot, High Salinity
Storage Layer

Absorbed Radiation

Bottom Loss

of water beds. In cold weather, the bags store heat for the house as the sun shines on them. At night or on cloudy days, they are protected from heat loss by an insulated panel. During hot weather, the steps are reversed. The bags of water are kept covered in the daylight hours. But at night, the panel is removed, during which time the bags are cooled and the heat from the interior of the house is lessened.

The plastic bag idea had its origins in a system that has been used for generations in rural areas: the *solar pond*. Shallow pools, filled with water, brine, and particles of dark rock or coal, absorb enough heat during the day to produce the equivalent of several kilowatts of heat. When the water is circulated to the interior of a nearby house, it will raise the temperature on cool days and assist the main heating system when the weather is cold.

As has been mentioned, mirrors have proven to be one of the most effective of all devices for capturing the energy of the sun. One of the most ambitious projects to be designed with mirrors was built in the early 1980s and called the "Power Tower," the largest installation of its kind ever built. The location was one of the sunniest in the United States, the Mojave Desert of California.

Picture an area covering one hundred acres—larger than ninety football fields placed together—in the shape of an oval bowl. This space was filled with mirrors on posts, resembling hundreds of small tables, encircling a central tower. When the mirrors were focused on the tower, concentrating the rays of the overhead sun, the structure began to glow, resembling some strange, gigantic lamp in the middle of the desert.

The tower was designed with a boiler, circulating one thousand gallons of water. As the heat intensified, this water turned into steam. Used to drive a turbine, the steam could generate enough electricity to supply a town of more than five thousand people—all from the sun.

Technologists have been developing another type of material and design that promises to be very effective in turning solar energy into power. This goes by the mystifying name of "evacuated tube collector." In effect, it is nothing more than one glass tube inside another glass tube, each separated from the other by a vacuum. The inner tube is painted black, in order to absorb more solar radiation. It then passes the heat to a central fluid-filled pipe, which circulates through the building that is to be heated.

EXAMPLES OF RADIANT ENERGY, DIRECT AND INDIRECT

Two terms are commonplace in describing solar energy systems. It is important to understand their differences.

(1) *Passive.* A system that is nonmechanical and utilizes no fuels, pumps, or fans. The installation described in the preceding section, using bags filled with water, is a good example of passive energy at work. In some cases, an entire home can be a passive solar collector. It might be constructed so that sunlight streams in from a southern exposure and warms the interior without use of fans or pumps. Attaching a greenhouse to a building is one way of attracting passive energy.

Although passive systems can never supply all of the solar energy needed for heating, they can supply as much as 40 percent. They are most effective when the building is located, of course, in a region where there is plenty of sunlight during cold weather and when the structure is positioned to face the sun. An efficient passive system can cut heating bills by about 25 percent, and in some cases, in half.

One device that has added to the effectiveness of a passive system is the "light shelf." Since sunlight rarely bathes a room evenly, additional heat can be obtained by mounting reflecting panels (or shelves) on windowsills. They bounce the sunlight into the darker areas of the room. Some builders have also made use of heat-retaining materials in walls that are exposed to the sun's rays. Such surfaces will continue radiating warmth long after the sunlight has vanished.

The *Trombe* wall, invented by an engineer who was a pioneer developer of solar furnaces, is a more complex and efficient kind of solar wall. It is really two walls in one: an outer layer of glass and an inner one of concrete painted black. As the sun warms the air between the concrete and the glass, the air rises and moves through vents. Cool air from inside the building is automatically drawn into vents in the bottom of the wall, where it continues the cycle.

Strange though it may seem, buildings can be *cooled* as well as heated through passive systems. An obvious method is the use of natural ventilation, designed so that breezes are sucked through the rooms that are to be cooled. But some buildings are now being equipped with roof sprayers. Water sprayed on a hot roof causes evaporation, which in turn dissipates the heat into the air and lowers the inside temperature by as much as ten or fifteen degrees. Sometimes, in very hot climates, the roof is actually a shallow pool of water, which evaporates and has the same cooling effect.

(2) *Active*. A system that uses the same basic elements as the passive one, but that also contains mechanical devices to increase or hasten the heating process. Such devices may include fans, pumps, valves, switches, sensors, motors, or combinations of two or more.

Active solar systems are most practical for buildings where the most important energy requirement is heating. This certainly includes residences in northern climes where heating accounts for as much as 75 percent of the annual fuel bill. It is less important in commercial buildings, where lighting and air conditioning consume as much as 70 percent of the energy input.

Active solar systems rely on collectors, the installations that first capture the sun's radiation. There are more than one hundred different

Clear vacuum tubes form the sun-capturing and insulating cover of a solar collector invented by General Electric. Laboratory tests indicate that this collector can absorb more solar heat than flat plate collectors.

types of collectors. The most common type, however, has long been the flat plate collector. Almost invariably it contains water or other liquid flowing through pipes and transfers heat to the area to be heated or to a storage tank.

Flat plate collectors come in many sizes and shapes. Tubular collectors function in much the same way. Their obvious drawback is that they function not at all during periods of darkness, and only poorly when sunlight is weak.

Two other important terms are used to describe the technology of solar energy:

(1) *Direct conversion.* This includes all forms of energy derived directly from sunlight itself that are either used immediately or stored for a brief period before use. The sun's energy might be captured by flat plate collectors, tubes, mirrors, water bags, solar cells, or any other devices and materials of the kinds already discussed.

(2) *Indirect conversion.* This term is used when energy is tapped from sources that originate with the sun's radiation but are not sunlight itself. Such sources include wind, ocean currents, flowing or falling water, and temperature differences in the waters of the seas.

The most widely used form of indirect conversion is hydroelectric power, or harnessing the water falling from dams and reservoirs.

Solar Cells & Solar Pioneers

PROMISING DISCOVERIES AND DEVICES

Harnessing the sun's rays directly can often be done in ways that are instantly visible, effective, and dramatic. A solar cooker is a good example. Simply a bowl-shaped, mirrored surface no larger than a circular outdoor grill, a solar cooker on a sunny day can boil water in a matter of minutes with no sign of smoke or flame.

A solar furnace is even more astonishing. In the small village of Mont-Louis in the French Pyrenees mountains a few years ago, one could have seen one of these installations at work. It operated on the same simple principle as the solar cooker and, indeed, resembled it—though on a gigantic scale. Banks of flat mirrors were positioned on a curving hillside, each one reflecting the sun's rays on a large mirror that consisted of 3,500 tiny mirrors forming a bowl. These concentrated rays were then focused on the furnace unit. On a bright day in Mont-Louis, which enjoys an average of 250 sunshiny days a year, the focus of the rays was intense enough to generate temperatures of more than 5,000 degrees Fahrenheit. Thick bars of iron melted in the solar furnace like so many sticks of butter—in about the same amount of time it takes to read this sentence.

THE SOLAR CELL

A more sophisticated device for harnessing the sun is the solar cell, which originated as the "photovoltaic cell." Most cameras today have

Car powered by 484 silicon solar cells placed over its cab. Electricity from the cells charges the battery at a speed of 11 miles an hour. On a sunny day the car can travel for six miles on one charge of electricity.

built-in light meters that adjust the lens or the shutter speed automatically. But the first light meters were hand-held instruments, with needles activated by the strength of sunlight striking photoelectric cells.

Light-sensitive cells of this kind were used in numerous experiments more than one hundred years ago. Scientists realized even then that there was an element of power—tiny though it was—that activated the cells. Yet, strangely enough, it was not until the early 1950s that inventors began devising ways of increasing and harnessing power from cells that were sensitive to light and activated by the sun.

The fact that sunlight could stimulate the flow of electricity in certain materials was considered a "scientific curiosity," largely because the wattage was so low. Then, in 1954, the Bell Telephone Laboratories began manufacturing much more powerful solar cells. Improved cells and combinations of cells were, for the first time, making it possible to use them to operate equipment that formerly had been driven by batteries or connections to electrical outlets.

In effect, solar cells are really batteries that never wear out and continue to function as long as there is enough sunlight available.

What are these devices and what do they look like?

A typical solar cell is a very thin wafer, about the size of a dime. In actuality, it is a slice from a rod made of silicon crystal mixed with impurities such as phosphorus and boron. One impurity makes it possible for the crystal to conduct *positive* electric charges. The other impurity allows it to conduct *negative* charges.

The combination is similar to an automobile battery with two poles—one positive, the other negative.

When units of light (called "photons") strike a solar cell, they stimulate positive and negative charges. This action starts an electric current flowing. The current can be used to light a bulb or power a small motor. When great quantities of solar cells are linked together, they obviously can power heavier equipment and larger motors. They can also produce heat or run cooling and refrigeration equipment.

Solar cells are made of silicon, a nonmetallic element that is second only to oxygen as the most common ingredient on earth. They convert light directly into electrical energy and can be used and reused indefinitely. Like batteries, they can be hooked together in a number of ways, but must be tightly connected so that their light-sensitive surfaces all face in one direction. Where space is limited, as in a satellite circling the globe, cells are occasionally "shingled." That is, they are arranged in overlapping squares, similar to the shingles on a roof.

Unlike batteries, however, solar cells are not available in a wide range of sizes. Furthermore, they are costly to manufacture because they have to be processed individually and cut and polished with great delicacy.

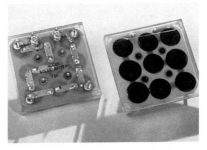

Collection of solar cells developed and tested at Bell Laboratories

The most basic form of commercial solar cell is a unit used to power a small transistor radio, operate other kinds of portable electronic equipment, and open garage doors that are activated by headlights from an automobile. More powerful combinations of cells can be found in battery-charging equipment and on lighted buoys along seacoast's or on rivers.

It will not be long, though, before solar cells are commonplace for powering many kinds of machines and pieces of equipment used around the house, in the yard, or for travel. That is because cells for the first time are being mass-produced. Eventually they will come down enough in cost so that they are economical to purchase as well as practical and convenient to use. Also, improvements in design and manufacture mean that fewer solar cells will be needed in the future to supply a given amount of power.

Even the shape of solar cells has been changing. Many are small, dime-like disks as described earlier, because it is relatively easy to mold rods of silicon and other substances and then slice them into wafers. But the trend is toward square or rectangular shapes, which can more easily be joined together to increase wattage or to fit readily into small areas where space is at a premium. In either case, the wafers are very thin.

One of the newest techniques is to manufacture the wafers in *sheets,* one step toward bringing down the cost and mass-producing the elements. These sheets can be cut into the most convenient and productive sizes to fit the equipment they will be energizing. Another manufacturing technique is to roll the cells out in continuous ribbons. Since the actual thickness of the cells is not important to their power or function, the ribbons can be made quite thin, thus cutting costs, saving time, and using minimum quantities of the basic materials. The ribbon method has a further advantage—greater mechanical strength and resistance to separation.

Rating solar cells is much more difficult than rating, say, a light bulb. Why? Because the output varies, depending upon the intensity of the sun or other light source involved. That's why scientists evolved a formula: The output of solar cells is given in peak watts, or amount of power a cell produces in full sunlight when the temperature is 77 degrees Fahrenheit. Though it may sound contradictory, the *higher* the temperature becomes (over about 80 degrees Fahrenheit), the *lower* the efficiency of the cell.

Solar cells have one other important characteristic. They are most efficient when they are close to the machinery or equipment they are powering. This means that "rooftop" installations are likely to be more effective and cheaper than central power banks that feed electricity from a cluster of cells to a number of outlying areas.

HOW SOLAR DEVICES FUNCTION IN ACTUAL PRACTICE

Many solar energy systems operate in remote areas of the globe, virtually unseen by human eyes for months on end. In the mountainous jungles of New Guinea, for example, solar cells power a vital telephone system that is largely unattended, except for routine annual inspections. The cells, drawing power from the sun, continually recharge the batteries of microwave relay stations.

Solar power has for some years been regularly used to supplement other power sources for telephone transmission lines in the United States, following experiments made in Georgia in 1955. And the military services have run tests with increasing frequency to provide field communications equipment that is entirely self-sufficient. The United States Army has also perfected solar units that will purify water, operate battlefront radar stations, and power emergency radios whether they are in the tropics or the Arctic.

Railroad companies for many years have been concerned about the more than 150,000 railroad crossings in the United States that have no protection except motionless signs. Now more and more crossings can be equipped with flashing lights, bells, and gates to warn of approaching trains. Although these systems obtain energy from the sun only during clear daylight hours, they require low wattage that can easily be stored during the interim periods when there is no sunlight.

The American highway system will be improved also, thanks to sun power. According to the National Safety Council, "the use of solar

Solar power is used to heat this tourist office in Wisconsin (above) and to operate railroad signals in remote areas (right).

energy will enable us to inaugurate a new era of highway safety.'' Automatic systems will help to guard vulnerable intersections, mountain curves and steep grades, and other sections of highway that are in remote sections where supervision and maintenance are difficult.

Navigational aids have benefited from the installation of batteries that can be recharged by the sun. Lighthouses, foghorns, bell buoys, and other warning devices can operate season after season, even during long periods of stormy weather when the sky is blanketed with clouds. The United States Coast Guard has tested many solar-powered navigational aids and discovered they can be relied on to continue functioning during the very worst storms, including those up to hurricane level.

Other kinds of warning systems are being developed to protect homes, public buildings, stores, and other properties from fire and theft. Solar power is used either directly or as a backup system in case the primary warning system breaks down.

A BOON TO ENVIRONMENTALISTS

Environmentalists have long been among the most outspoken supporters of solar power—and with good reason. Unlike coal or oil, solar energy creates no air or water pollutants. Unlike nuclear power, solar power invokes no threat of harmful radiation.

43

But environmentalists have yet another reason to be thankful for the kind of technology that is harnessing the sun. Solar cells have provided an excellent means of supplying constant, reliable power for ecology stations where automatic instruments can be installed to monitor pollution levels. They keep the instruments functioning day in and day out and also operate radio equipment, either on command or whenever pollution levels rise to the danger point.

SOLAR PIONEERS

The names of some early scientists who tried to harness the sun have for the most part been lost in the pages of history. Many failed in their ambitious dreams to have the sun accomplish great things for mankind. Others were obscured by the more notable achievements of their peers in other fields of science.

One of the first solar scientists whose work was recognized was a French engineer, Salomon de Caus. During the seventeenth century he invented several solar machines, including a small water pump run entirely by the sun. He is also said to have astonished a public gathering by demonstrating how mirrors could set cloth on fire at a distance of fifteen or twenty feet.

Salomon de Caus

In Germany during the same period, Athanasius Kircher was experimenting with a solar furnace, which he later described in a published article. The records show he was able to melt wax and lead and to distill water in a jar by focusing the sun's rays on it.

The famous French chemist Antoine Laurent Lavoisier, the founder of modern chemistry, was the first to design a successful solar furnace. Before he died in 1794, he had constructed several such furnaces, one of which could generate some 3,000 degrees Fahrenheit and melt metals. It consisted of two large lenses and the furnace unit, mounted on a wheeled platform that could be turned to catch the sun.

More than a century ago, one of the most ambitious solar energy projects ever conceived was designed by an American, Charles Wilson, for operation at Las Salinas, in the Atacama Desert of northern Chile. This was an immense distillation plant, turning salt water into fresh for use at one of the country's nitrate mines. The still consisted of hundreds of panes of glass slanted over shallow pans of salt water. Heat from the sun, which is constant in this South American desert, formed vapor on the inside of the slanting glass. The vapor then ran off in the form of fresh water and was collected in troughs for use.

At the Paris World's Fair in 1867 this artificial sun demonstrated how sunlight could be trapped and used for industrial purposes.

Wilson's solar venture was so successful, collecting more than five thousand gallons of fresh water a day, that it continued in operation for forty years. It might have continued even longer, functioning at practically no cost, had not the nitrate mine finally closed down.

The World Exposition in Paris in 1878 displayed several solar inventions. One of the most ingenious and practical was a solar steam engine devised by a printer, Able Pifre. Although the 100-foot solar collector, shaped like a dish, was able to generate only a single horsepower, that was sufficient to run a small printing press. Pifre exhibited his machine at the exposition by publishing *Le Journal du Soleil* (*The Sun Journal*).

Another French inventor, Auguste Mouchot, also had an exhibit at the exposition. This was a solar oven in which he cooked a pound of beef in twenty-five minutes.

In the United States, one of the most noted pioneers was Dr. Charles Greeley Abbot, who is referred to as the father of solar energy research in America. He did not come onto the scene, however, until the 1930s, when he experimented with solar stoves and boilers. His objective was not so much to create new inventions as to use the devices to study the nature and power of the sun's rays. A brilliant astrophysicist, Dr. Abbot conducted many solar experiments at the Smithsonian Institution in Washington, D.C. He also studied and cataloged various types of spectra and emissions from the sun, making a valuable contribution to the entire science of solar energy.

Most of the solar pioneers after the 1930s were groups of specialists working as teams, some for the government and some for private industry. Their accomplishments, therefore, are recorded in the names of organizations rather than individuals, such as Bell Telephone Laboratories, NASA, and the Association for Applied Solar Energy. One exception was Dr. Maria Telkes, who experimented with solar devices that could be used in emergency situations. Included among these were solar batteries, signal lights, and other equipment placed in survival kits ordered by the United States Navy. These were used by survivors of ships sunk during the war, as well as by pilots whose planes were shot down over water.

Using Solar Power Today

PUTTING THE SUN TO GOOD USE IN THE HOME

"Con Edison is offering solar water heating systems for 700 homes in New York City and Westchester County. The solar equipment should deliver virtually all the hot water that is needed in summer and about half of the year-round hot water needs. The total price for the system is $3,600. . . ."

This announcement, published in a leaflet distributed by the Consolidated Edison Company of New York in the early 1980s, characterizes the efforts being made by large utilities to bring solar power to their customers. As the leaflet also pointed out, the government offers special tax credits for citizens who invest in solar energy. That fact, plus a low electricity rate for backup water heating, said Con Edison, "helps make solar energy systems economically attractive for those who now heat water with electricity or oil."

Solar-assisted water heating systems of this kind are suited best to single-family homes with one or two stories and with sloping roofs that face south and are not shaded between mid-morning and mid-afternoon.

HOW THE SOLAR WATER HEATER WORKS

In an installation of this type, two collector panels on the roof capture the sun's heat and transport it in a closed-loop system (called a "solar loop") to a stone-lined 120-gallon tank where the home's hot

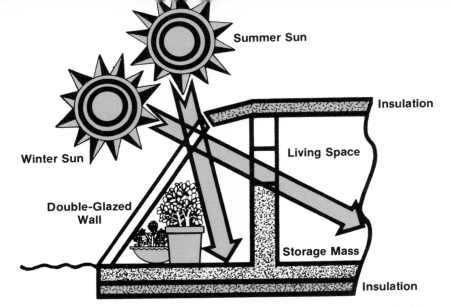

Summer Sun

Insulation

Winter Sun

Living Space

Double-Glazed Wall

Storage Mass

Insulation

An attached sun space, such as a greenhouse, can provide heat to a building. A heavy masonry wall and/or containers of water exposed to the sunlight will retain heat. This heat later can be delivered to the main building through doors, windows, or vents.

water is stored. A device in the bottom of this tank, called a "heat exchanger," transfers the heat from the solar loop to the domestic water supply.

Backup water heating is provided electrically on cloudy or rainy days when the solar panels do not provide enough heat. However, the electrical element operates only during nights or weekends, "low-peak" periods when the electricity rate is very low. The storage tank is large enough so that it can retain sufficient hot water during this interim.

Most experts seem to agree that the *home* is where we will see the most practical and extensive developments in solar energy, at least until the late 1990s. Hot water heating (as the Con Edison program demonstrates) is already practical, despite the high initial cost. The savings obtained from using free energy from the sun will gradually wipe out the expense of installing a solar water heater.

The second most practical application for the home lies in solar *heating*. The initial installations are costly, but the eventual savings are great—especially when the ever-increasing rates for fuel oil, natural gas, and electricity are considered.

A typical heating system works in this manner: Solar panels are installed on a slanted roof that faces south. As the air in the panels heats up, it is pumped through insulated ducts to the basement. There the hot air is retained for long periods of time in a solar box containing as much as two tons of stones. As heat is needed in various parts of the house, the hot air from the storage box is released gradually. The movement of air is carefully regulated by thermostats in each room.

Depending, of course, upon the outside temperature, the solar box can store enough heat to last two or three days, should there be a period of rain or cloudy weather. Unless the house is in a southern clime where heat requirements are low, a backup heating system is used whenever solar energy fails to meet the demand.

Another common system uses water pipes in the collector on the roof. Instead of hot air, the heated water is circulated to a storage tank in the basement. The house can then be heated by either of two methods: hot water circulation through the rooms, or hot air from pipes that run through the water storage tank. A solar system in the home is usually more efficient and more economical in the long run when it is used concurrently for both space heating and hot water.

THE ULTIMATE IN SOLAR HOMES

The systems described above are relatively low-cost and are designed for modest single-family homes, old or new. But what can a builder accomplish if he installs a complex solar system that incorporates the latest materials and devices?

One pioneer in this field, Harry F. Thomason, built three such homes in the 1960s and 1970s with the idea of supplying 90 percent of heating needs from the sun. From the standpoint of solar efficiency, they were the most successful homes built up to that time. One house, in the Washington, D.C., area, used a 1,600-gallon tank of hot water surrounded by insulating stones. The water was stored after flowing through pipes in a collector that covered most of the southern slant of the roof. The house was heated by air circulated through the hot stones and up into the various rooms. This system was so effective that one home's auxiliary heating system consumed less than ten gallons of fuel oil during an entire winter!

Crystal Pavilion built by M.I.T.

Many families overlook the fact that *windows* themselves can be very effective elements in a solar energy system. "The secret lies in developing your *existing* windows as solar-heat collectors," says Edward Allen, associate professor of architecture at M.I.T., "and in operating these window collectors efficiently during the winter months. It's neither difficult nor expensive."

Allen suggests making a chart of all window areas over a period of time, determining which ones let in sunlight and for how long on a typical winter day. In most cases, it is easy to open curtains and draperies in sunny windows and close them at night. Windows that are never sunny should be more heavily curtained, even if they have double layers of glass.

"In planning a new construction," advises Allen, "there are significant energy savings to be realized over the lifetime of buildings by orienting most windows to the south, and by providing them with summer shading devices. In any dwelling, new or old, there's a good feeling that comes from knowing that you and Mother Nature are working together as closely as possible to keep your house cozy."

People who like to grow plants can derive extra benefits from building a small greenhouse on the south side of their home, provided they live in climates that are either warm or temperate. Besides providing energy for growing plants, the sunlight can be captured and stored in much the same way as through a roof collector. An interesting phenomenon is the "greenhouse effect," which is explained in this manner: Since glass is transparent to the sun's *short wave-length* rays, these rays pass right through and warm the floors and walls inside. But the rays that are emitted from the heated walls and floors are now *infrared*. Having longer wave lengths, the infrared rays will not pass back out through the glass.

Bear in mind that solar power can be used to *cool* homes as well as to heat them, although it will not be until the 1990s that practical, low-cost solar air conditioners will be available to home owners. The cooling power of the sun is discussed later in this book.

THE SUN AT WORK IN BUSINESS AND INDUSTRY

Today we are witnessing the growth of a whole new industry in America, one that will not really be firmly established much before the year 2000. But we have already started to reap its benefits.

"Solar energy," reported the American Petroleum Institute in a recent evaluation of solar energy industries, "includes a variety of energy technologies which derive energy directly from the sun . . . as well as those which derive energy indirectly." The report went on to say that the solar field began to look particularly attractive to American industries and businesses during the late 1970s when the prices of oil and gas began to rise alarmingly.

Manufacturers of a wide variety of consumer products have been getting into the solar field. An increasing number of items for sale in stores use solar cells, among them such products as wristwatches, calculators, portable radios, and electronic games. They contain light-transforming wafers of silicon that generate electricity from the sunlight, even though they may be exposed to this energy source very briefly from time to time.

Solar batteries are supplying electricity for agricultural and commercial equipment that can function unattended for weeks and months on end. One interesting example is a series of remote meteorological observation stations powered entirely by solar panels at their base. They provide weather information twenty-four hours a day. A unique application of solar power can be seen on certain types of metal bridges on American highways. The bridges are equipped with solar panels whose only function is to transmit weak electrical currents through the steel girders. The currents help to prevent corrosion in the metal.

It used to be that the more remote the area, the more likely it was that solar cells could be found functioning in silent solitude. But that situation is changing as the costs gradually come down and solar power is able to compete in the marketplace with other forms of energy. Solar cells are becoming popular among commercial farmers, who use them for pumping water, preventing ice from forming on ponds where livestock drink in the winter, supplying outbuildings with temporary lighting, or supplementing heaters in barns.

The petroleum industry has found numerous valuable uses for solar power, particularly on oil wells in wilderness regions and on drilling rigs at sea. In the Gulf of Mexico, for example, automated and unmanned platforms rely more and more on solar panels. The panels generate the power needed to operate the control systems for wells producing oil and gas. Solar energy also supplies power for navigational lights on these rigs.

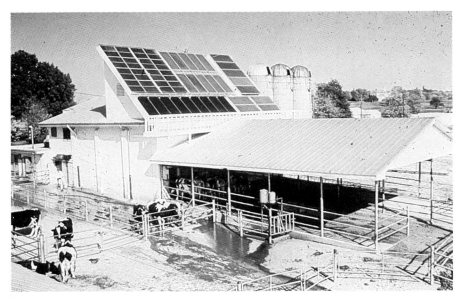

Solar dairy barn

SUNNY CALIFORNIA

It is not surprising that much of the early commercial development of solar energy occurred in California. The state had the right combination of sunshine, industry, and financing to undertake the research and engineering necessary. It also offered (and still does) the largest tax credits in the country to encourage the widespread use of solar energy. As a result, California at one time had nearly one third of all the solar energy systems installed in the United States. These ranged from heated swimming pools to residential heating units, a large commercial laundry, fruit drying facilities, wine fermentation vats, and a soup and vegetable cannery.

The city of Santa Clara, situated in a sunny valley some fifty miles south of San Francisco, is a good example of what one community can do to hasten the ultimate harnessing of the sun. Realizing that the area enjoyed about three hundred days a year with clear skies, the city administrators started the solar age with the construction of a community recreation building that could rely on the sun for more than 80 percent of its energy. That included cooling as well as heating.

"What we see is a city-owned solar utility," said the city manager at the time of the construction in 1975. "We will finance and install solar heating and cooling systems in new buildings. Consumers will pay a monthly fee to cover maintenance and amortization of the solar units. This will be done on a nonprofit basis, with the capital raised from municipal bonds."

Other states and other communities also have seen the potential for solar energy and made plans accordingly. In Atlanta, Georgia Power Company took the lead by designing a new headquarters building that would derive one third of its heating, air conditioning, and hot water from the sun. To do so required the design of some 28,000 square feet of solar concentrators, at a cost that would not be made up in energy savings for about fifteen years. But the power company saw this as a "visible symbol of its interest in solar energy" and estimated that solar energy would supply 5 percent of its total generation by the end of the century.

To critics who said that solar energy was all right in the South and Southwest but not in more northerly parts of America, the U.S. Department of Energy replied, "If you're starting with a new structure, there's absolutely no reason you can't have a system that's cost-effective in New Hampshire, Vermont, and other areas with relatively little sunshine."

In fact, two federal government buildings were recently designed to use solar energy for both heating and cooling. One of the building sites is in New Hampshire; the other is in Michigan. In addition, the National Science Foundation began funding and testing a variety of solar energy buildings across the country. One is a $10 million educational center at the Denver Community College in Colorado. It was estimated that the solar plant for heating the center would pay for itself in ten years. This took into account the cost of conventional fuels versus the negligible cost of the solar energy system.

Other major solar projects include a conservatory and administration building for the New York Botanical Garden in Milbrook, New York; a library for the Audubon Society in Lincoln, Massachusetts; and a forty-story skyscraper in Pittsburgh.

According to the National Science Foundation, the solar heating and cooling of major business and industrial buildings will be "economically competitive" in most regions of the United States by the early 1990s. They already are commercially practical in America's Sunbelt states.

SOLAR TRANSPORTATION

Solar energy is in its infancy and, with respect to transportation, will be for many years. A few individuals and organizations are experimenting in this field. But the problem is the difficulty in designing a solar collector that will stay in focus on the sun while in motion.

Nevertheless, several inventors have designed electric automobiles that are sun powered. One, the Baker electric car, described as "the world's first sun-powered automobile," has a collecting panel on top

The *Solar Challenger*, powered by the solar cells on its wings, flew across the English Channel in 1981 and made history.

that is as large as the roof itself. The vehicle, though slow and cumbersome, *does move* when the sun is out. Another vehicle resembles an enclosed golf cart, topped by a slanting panel made up of almost five hundred solar cells. It can travel six miles at slow speed on a day-long charging in the sun.

Aircraft would seem to be natural choices for solar energy assistance, since they so often operate in sunlight above the clouds, even on the stormiest of days. Indeed, experiments have been made with solar power for in-flight use and will undoubtedly bring about future developments.

One of the most dramatic aeronautical successes was the *Solar Challenger*, a unique aircraft powered only by solar cells. The craft made aviation history in July 1981, when it flew across the English Channel in a little more than five hours. Solar cells on the wings provided electricity for turning two three-horsepower motors for the propellers.

THE MAGICAL COOLING POWER OF THE SUN

Solar heating has long been thought of as a practical way to harness the sun. But *cooling*—that is a different story, one that almost seems contradictory.

The very air conditioning units that are so familiar to us, though, are powered by the sun in a roundabout way. For the oil, coal, or natural gas that is used today to produce electricity had its origins in the sun millions of years ago.

Solar coolers can be designed to extract the heat from homes and other buildings by simply reversing the cycle that produces heat. Water or other fluid is circulated through the system at night so that it loses its heat and becomes cool. During the daytime, the cool liquid is then run through the system to keep the inside of the building cool. By this time, the storage tank or rocks in the basement have themselves become cool and can be counted on to remain cool for twelve hours or more.

If the system uses air instead of water, the air is circulated past the cool water tank or rocks in the basement and then up into the interior of the building.

These two techniques have limitations and are useful only in regions where the climate is not too hot and the need for cooling is moderate. They are examples of *passive* solar cooling. They can be supplemented by several other nonmechanical methods as well, such as:

• *Night sky radiation*. A roof is covered with a heavy layer of material or water. It absorbs heat from the building below and in turn radiates the heat to the cooler night sky. During the day, the material on the roof is covered with an insulating material or shaded by the positioning of large trees.

• *Ground cooling*. Since the ground is nearly always cooler than the air, the more a building is in contact with the earth around it, the cooler it will be in hot weather. Setting a building into the side of a hill or mounding earth as high as is practical around the foundation is the simplest method to obtain more cool ground contact. Drawing air into a building from pipes in the ground will accomplish much the same results.

• *Thick wall construction*. If the floors and walls of a building are constructed of heavy materials such as stone, brick, or clay, they will cool down at night and absorb the heat inside the house during the day. That is why even the simplest dwellings in remote villages in Africa or South America are constructed of thick adobe or mud.

MECHANICAL AIR CONDITIONING

In large buildings and in regions where seasons can be very hot, passive cooling is not sufficient. In such cases, or where more critical control must be maintained over interior temperatures, *mechanical air conditioning* is required. Yet this too can be powered by the sun. In fact, many experts state that solar air conditioning offers certain advantages over solar heating because the sun is more powerful during the hot seasons when the energy is most needed.

Cost is now—and will be for many years—the biggest drawback to solar cooling, though it is gradually coming down toward the levels of air conditioning with conventional fuels.

One of the most practical methods today is called the *absorption cooler*. The system includes this series of units and functions:

• A *solar collector* on the roof, similar to one used for heating a building and, indeed, usable for either heating or cooling. Liquid in the collector is heated by the sun and then circulated through the next element, a generator.

• A *generator*, containing a liquid which becomes vaporized when heated by the liquid from the roof. The vapor then circulates to the condenser.

• A *condenser*. Here the heat is removed from the vapor, which then changes to a cooled liquid. The liquid is then revaporized through an *expansion valve*, and passes into an evaporator.

• An *evaporator*, made up of coils through which the cool vapor passes.

• An *absorber*, into which the cool vapor then passes from the evaporator.

When warm air from the rooms in a building is blown over the cooling coils of the evaporator, it is cooled to about 70 degrees Fahrenheit and then recirculated through the rooms.

Kisii village huts in Nairobi, Kenya. The thick walls of these huts absorb heat during the day and cool down at night.

This oversimplified explanation demonstrates how the heat from the sun can trigger a process that results in cooler air. Among the factors that make the process possible are differences in pressure in the various units that help in changing liquids to vapors. Of equal importance is the nature of the liquids in the various elements, which act as refrigerants—just as they do in a refrigerator or any standard air conditioning unit.

Another type of solar air conditioner is known as the *Rankine Cycle*. Solar energy is captured and intensified through one of several methods of the kind already described for heating water and making steam. The steam is then used to turn a small turbine. The turbine can either drive a conventional air conditioner or else turn a generator and make electricity.

At night or on rainy and cloudy days, the air conditioner is run by the building's regular electric current. In some systems, however, especially those in remote locations, the electricity manufactured by the sun can be stored in batteries for use at any time.

Using the sun to keep us cool as well as warm is very expensive today. Yet in the not-too-distant future it will become commonplace to think of solar energy as a better and more economical means of air conditioning, and even as a power source for refrigerators and freezers.

Solar Storage Systems & Jobs

DEVICES AND EQUIPMENT FOR STORING SOLAR ENERGY

When a conventional furnace is used to heat your home, you never have to worry about *storing* the heat as long as you have plenty of fuel oil, natural gas, or coal. The furnace is designed to click on and off according to the setting on the thermostat. This system will work perfectly well with a solar heating system—*as long as the sun is shining*. But when night falls or the sky clouds over, the heating cycle slows down and then ceases altogether.

There are two ways in which the heating process can be continued, though only for a limited amount of time:

• In a *passive* solar-heating system, the heat will continue to radiate if it has been absorbed by the thick walls and floors of the building.

• In an *active* system, mechanical means are used to circulate air through the large water tank or rocks in the basement that have been absorbing the heat from the collector on the roof. Sometimes there is enough heat in these storage facilities to supply the heating requirements of the building for a couple of days. The size of the storage and the temperature outside will, of course, determine how quickly the heat must be used up to maintain the interior at a comfortable level.

It requires a large storage tank and hundreds of gallons of water to supply the needs of a modest-sized home and maintain the right temperature during several cloudy days. This means that a certain amount of space in the basement must be sacrificed for the purpose. Solar engineers have long pondered the question: Are there other substances besides ordinary water and rocks that will store more heat more efficiently in the same amount of space?

Industrial researchers have experimented with a number of chemicals, both liquid and solid, as well as with particles of metal, coal, asphalt, and ceramic clays. Some have proved to be only a little more efficient. Others have been too costly or scarce for practical purposes.

One of the prime candidates is sodium sulfate, a crystalline substance long used in the manufacture of soaps, detergents, and dyes. Sometimes called Glauber's salt after the seventeenth century chemist who discovered it, it has proven itself in heating tests. A container holding only 150 cubic feet of the salt is as effective as a tank holding more than 1,000 cubic feet of water. Sodium sulfate will hold as much heat over a reasonable period of time as fifteen times the same cubic footage of rocks.

Researchers have noted that an interesting change takes place in this substance during the course of absorbing and giving off heat. As the sun's heat streams to the salt from the collector on the roof, it changes from crystals to a semiliquid, somewhat gluelike in consistency. This change apparently causes the substance to absorb much more heat than is possible with water, rocks, or most other materials.

This salt-gradient pond at Argonne National Laboratory is used for heat storage. Sunlight is trapped at the pond's lower levels for later use.

When the procedure is reversed and the salt starts to transfer its heat back into the rooms of a building, it turns back into a solid.

Scientists at M.I.T. have been trying to determine the significance of the change from liquid to solid, whether for sodium sulfate or any other materials. Experimenting with similar chemicals for use in radiator panels, they discovered that the same principle worked in the transfer of heat. By alternating between a liquid and a solid, the chemicals absorbed or discharged heat more efficiently than did substances that underwent no such change.

Researchers have also looked into the possibility of using chemicals in coils of pipes in the solar collector on the roof. If certain liquids proved to absorb the heat more effectively or more quickly than water, they could increase the temperatures of the storage facilities in the basement. Thus it would not be necessary to circulate such large quantities from the storage units at any given time.

SOLAR "RESERVOIRS"

Some large public utilities in the United States have used an ingenious method to cope with peak demands on electricity and even out the flow of current to customers. During the early morning hours when people are asleep and homes are dark, the utilities continue generating electricity but use the surplus to pump water into reservoirs several hundred feet above the power generation plants. Then when the demand for electricity is high, at supper time and during the earlier part of the evening, the reservoir gates are opened. The water flows downward, turning the turbines and generating electricity.

Solar energy can be used in much the same way. When the sun is shining brightly, solar power is used to pump water into a reservoir. Then, during hours of darkness or on cloudy days, the force of the water flowing from the reservoir can be tapped in much the same way as is done by the public utilities.

This method obviously is impractical for use in individual homes or buildings. Yet it could be a practical way of capturing the sun's energy to heat a large industrial complex or homes in an entire community.

THE CHALLENGE OF MORE EFFICIENT STORAGE

"It is a fact of solar energy technology that storage is the big handicap. Until an effective, inexpensive method of storing collected heat overnight or during overcast days is found, solar energy as a viable alternative power source may be a long time coming."

This statement, made by a specialist in a report on solar energy at the beginning of the 1980s, has been echoed by most of the engineers working in this field. Although they generally agree that water storage tanks and bins filled with rocks can adequately fill the modest needs of small homes, they emphasize that much better methods and more efficient materials are badly needed.

Looking at the situation from the standpoint of business and industry, *Business Week* magazine reported, "In the long run, the usefulness and economies of any solar system may depend as much on storage technology as on collection and conversion technology."

This statement brings into focus the changing nature of man's attempts to harness the sun. Not so many years ago, scientists and engineers devoted most of their time to perfecting rooftop collectors and methods of transferring the heat from one place to another. Now they are wrestling with the storage problem, which has gradually come to be recognized as the biggest roadblock.

A major objective is to get heat to the basement storage system more quickly and consequently with less heat loss. One method incorporates the use of a *heat pump*. This is based on a device that is commonly used in ordinary kitchen refrigerators. The value of the heat pump is that it removes heat from the air—even from air that would be described as very cold.

Have you ever noticed the family cat hugging the bottom of the refrigerator? That is because the animal likes the heat that flows through the vents at floor level. You can feel the warmth with your hand. The heat pump is extracting warm air from the refrigerator and making the inside colder. The excess heat is, in this case, exhausted as useless, though there is no reason why it could not be stored or circulated elsewhere in the house.

Technician checks solar panels used to generate electricity on a natural gas platform in the Gulf of Mexico.

A heat pump attached to a solar energy system will accomplish the same thing—removing residues of heat as the air flows to the storage area. By increasing the heat derived from a solar-collecting system, the pump also makes it possible to use smaller storage facilities.

THE SOLAR HEAT PIPE

At a recent exhibit of solar-heating devices, visitors at one booth were asked to hold in one hand a short piece of metal pipe, sealed at both ends. It was cold to the touch. Then they were instructed to immerse one end in a pan of hot water on a small burner. Within less than half a minute the whole pipe would become so hot that the participant would have to drop it hastily.

What happened? How could a few inches of hot water in a pan have generated that much heat up and down the metal?

The answer is that this was a sample of a *solar heat pipe,* in reality a very simple device that may have important applications in solar heating. Inside the pipe was a small amount of liquid such as ammonia or even ordinary water. When the bottom of the pipe was heated, the liquid quickly changed to vapor, rising up the length of the pipe and then condensing into a liquid again, to be reheated. This cycle works well—and quickly—because the pressure inside the sealed pipe is much lower than the atmospheric pressure outside. Under these conditions, liquids vaporize much more quickly and at much lower temperatures than normal boiling points.

Solar heat pipes would accomplish two important things in a solar-heating cycle. First, they would convey far more heat than water pipes to the storage facility. Second, they would speed up the cycle so that a solar-heating system would absorb far more energy during the day than would otherwise be possible.

These are but a few of the types of challenges that are being met when it comes to the storage and transmittal of energy from the sun.

RELATED TECHNOLOGIES AND CAREERS

As one personnel manager and career adviser said in a talk to a group of students, ''I predict sunny weather for young people who are planning to enter the solar energy field.'' He pointed out that there is nowhere such a career could go but *up*. As for the economic problems of getting solar energy installations into common use, these challenges only seem to accelerate the need for engineers, designers, and other specialists who can hasten the development.

The following examples of job specifications will give you a better idea of the people who are needed to get solar energy into high gear between now and the end of the century:

• *Solar scientists*. They come from a variety of scientific backgrounds, some with a knowledge of other energy forms, such as oil or coal, some versed in meteorology and oceanography. Fundamentally, these are the men and women who become involved with research projects, both in the field and in university laboratories.

• *Solar engineers*. Most have basic engineering degrees, with special studies in heating and cooling or building construction and planning. They go beyond the theories of the researchers and work with applications and installations.

• *Solar technicians*. These people do not necessarily have college degrees, but have studied solar technology, as well as some engineering. They tend to work as assistants to engineers. Some may work part-time while studying for a degree program.

• *Solar-heating consultants.* For the most part, this group is made up of men and women in business for themselves, or perhaps working with two or three partners. Most likely, they were general consultants who began to study the expanding solar field and saw a need. They act as advisers, often bringing in architects, engineers, or other specialists with whom they maintain regular contact.

• *Architects.* Most architects and building designers today know a great deal about passive solar energy installations. But there are some who specialize in both passive and active solar design. One of their most important objectives is to attain a good balance of efficiency and beauty—a challenging task sometimes, since solar collectors can be ugly and cumbersome on a large building.

• *Solar equipment technologists.* As in every part of the building and planning field, there are specialists who have detailed information about equipment and installations and their comparative costs and availability. These people work closely with builders and architects who know what is needed but may not have the latest information on manufacturers, design specifications, range of capabilities, or costs.

• *Salespersons.* This group is made up of men and women who may be in real estate or who are simply marketing solar equipment on behalf of certain manufacturers. They may be selling solar-equipped homes and other buildings, complete installations, or individual products.

• *Computer programmers and operators.* Since solar energy is new, complex, and competitive with other forms of energy, there is an ever-growing need for computers to calculate the short-range and long-range facts. These might relate to performance and efficiency or to the economics of solar installations.

• *Government representatives.* Federal, state, and local governments are increasingly concerned with the study and administration of solar energy programs. They need people who can supervise and coordinate the planning of solar projects at all levels.

Cost Of Solar Systems

THE ECONOMICS OF SOLAR POWER

The United States Department of Energy (DOE) estimated in 1983 that solar energy will be providing 10 percent or less of America's total energy needs by the year 2000.

Why is this estimate so low? We have already seen that solar technology is advancing rapidly and that there are many advantages to solar power, not the least of which is that there is almost no pollution or damage to the environment.

Despite insistent comments that the sun's rays are universal and *free,* the problem is an economic one. The rays may be free, but the methods and installations necessary to convert solar energy to man's use are not. Passive solar heating is the least expensive, but also the least effective. Using the sun's energy to generate electricity is both complex and costly, about ten times as much as the average utility rate for domestic electricity.

For this reason, the Electric Power Research Institute is even more conservative in its estimate than the DOE, predicting that electricity from the sun would be less than 5 percent by the year 2000.

THE COST TO HOME OWNERS

In terms of actual dollars spent for a solar-heating installation for a new home, builders estimate a total cost increase of 10 to 15 percent. Thus, a $100,000 house would have an investment of $10,000 to

Aerial view of a solar farm collector system (above). Technician (right) assembles photovoltaic cells that can convert sunlight directly into electricity.

$15,000 in solar heating and hot water. This estimate is for a climate that experiences winter with a moderate amount of snow and cold weather. But it does not take into account the fact that a conventional heating system must also be installed as a backup.

Why should the expense be that high? The basic solar materials are substantial, including more than 700 square feet of solar collectors for a modest 3,000-square-foot home and thirty thousand pounds of stone for storing heat. In addition, the system requires a large tank, a network of pipes, controls, extra insulation, and preferably thicker walls and floors.

One architect's estimate stated that it would take about five years for a solar-heating system to supply as much useful energy as it took to supply the materials and build the installation itself.

Owners of solar energy installations point out that once the system has been installed, it immediately begins to pay for itself in terms of energy costs that are saved. The statement is true, but the initial cost might not be amortized for twelve to fifteen years. And by that time, the installation itself might need renovation and improving.

Our real hope is for the future, when entire communities will have their own centrally located solar power plants. Home owners in those locations would benefit immensely because they would avoid the high installation and start-up costs. They would pay for the service, but the costs would be moderate, much less than for fuel oil, coal, or natural gas. Also, they would reap the benefit of more efficient storage facilities—ones that might continue to supply power during a whole week of cloudy and rainy weather.

Solar installatons offer another strong incentive: tax reductions and credits for individuals, families, and businesses that pay for them. Such credits are usually offered by state, local, and federal governments and can add up to substantial amounts.

COMBINATIONS OF ENERGY, SOLAR AND OTHER

An old song has a line that starts off "Sunshine on my shoulders makes me happy. . . ." There is certainly something about the sun that lifts the spirits. And solar power is no exception. When a solar energy system is working at its peak, stimulated by the rays of the brightly shining sun, it seems to offer something beyond simply heat and hot water.

But when night comes or banks of clouds close down the sky, users of solar energy systems have to face the reality that they just might need an alternate form of power. In most cases, they can count on stored energy to do the job—but only for a while. Then they must rely on *alternate energy,* some kind of backup system.

It is helpful to know something about the other kinds of energy available, since all forms of energy can work in partnership. Some— like solar energy—work best when combined with other forms. Oil, coal, and natural gas are referred to as "conventional" fuels, simply because they have become most commonplace and widespread throughout the civilized world. But other forms of energy are vital, and in some locations are more important than the primary fuels. These are the ones you should be familiar with:

Nuclear. This type of energy can be used only by major utilities to generate electricity. In the process, uranium is used instead of fuel oil or coal to heat water into steam. As the uranium atoms split apart in a reactor, enormous quantities of heat are released. This heat forms the steam that drives turbines, which then produce electricity.

Water from this geothermal well in Hawaii (left) is almost fit to drink. Geothermal energy is a natural source of power. Nuclear energy is powerful. Each one of the 217 fuel bundles in the fuel core (above) can provide the energy equivalent of 326 railroad hopper cars of coal.

Nuclear power is one of the major energy sources available in almost limitless quantities to produce power for generations to come. The same cannot be said of oil or natural gas, which are in limited supply and must be conserved.

Geothermal. Like solar energy, geothermal energy is a natural source of power that is clean and almost totally free of pollutants. It can best be described as natural heat captured by fluids trapped in rock formations thousands of feet below the surface of the earth. In most regions, this molten rock lies far too deep to be reached and tapped in any practical manner. But in some places, the heat has worked its way close to the surface. If you have ever visited Yellowstone Park, you have seen visual evidence of geothermal energy in the form of hot springs, geysers, or fumaroles—holes in the earth through which vapors and hot gases rise.

The largest and most successful geothermal project in America is at the Geysers Geothermal Field in northern California. This has a deep reservoir of dry steam. It is estimated that generators powered by this natural flow of steam could one day supply electricity for a city of more than two million people. On a nationwide basis, geothermal

Supplementary energy sources include biomass, such as wood chips (left). Wind-powered turbines (above) can be used as alternate energy sources in an oil field.

sources in the United States could supply as much energy each day as almost one million barrels of crude oil.

Biomass. This term is one of the least known in the energy field. Nevertheless, many newspapers have published articles about plans to burn garbage to produce power. Biomass includes not only garbage and trash but also sawdust, wood chips, corn stalks, and other waste materials. As you can see, this method accomplishes two goals at the same time: supplying energy and cleaning up the environment.

Some of this organic matter can be processed with chemicals and heat to produce liquid fuels such as alcohols, fuel oil, and "gasohol," which has been used successfully to run automobiles for many years. Other waste materials that are not so easily processed would simply be formed into pellets of various sizes to be burned like logs.

Biomass, which could be used to supplement solar power, is actually an indirect form of solar energy. The sun's energy, stored as chemical energy in the organic plant life that makes up biomass, can be converted into the types of fuels mentioned and accomplish the same power goals.

Synthetic. Have you ever heard of gasoline made from coal? Or oil squeezed from a rock? Or natural gas formed from tar? These are all possible in today's energy world and are just three of many products known as *synthetic fuels*. The word *synthetic* does not mean there is anything fake or unnatural about these fuels. Rather, it denotes that certain types of fuels have been converted into other types, mainly because they are more useful and practical in the new forms.

Research into the conversion of coal into gasoline came about, for example, when America faced dwindling supplies of oil. Potential supplies of coal are large enough to last for the next four or five hundred years, although the outlook for oil is perhaps one tenth of that.

Synthetics can also come from more direct sources, two of which are *oil shale* and *tar sands*. Shale actually looks like rock. Yet under a microscope, what seems to be solid rock actually contains very tiny specks of kerogen, or partially formed oil. The oil can be extracted through processes that are still complicated and expensive, and used the same ways as crude oil that flows from wells.

Tar sands are saturated with an oily, tarry substance. Tremendous deposits of these sands are found in Utah in their natural state. They can be extracted by injecting the deep deposits with steam. The tar is thus melted to a liquid, which can be pumped to the surface through heated pipes and processed into oil and gasoline.

In the early twenty-first century, says the Energy Research and Development Administration (ERDA), America will no longer be able to rely on one or two resources for the bulk of its energy. This has periodically been done throughout U.S. history, first with wood, later with coal, and today with oil.

By the year 2025, six energy sources, none supplying more than 25 percent of the total, may power the nation. These resources are nuclear, solar, geothermal and hydroelectric power, coal, petroleum, and natural gas.

By that time, six facets of solar technology will meet almost one quarter of the total energy demand: solar-heated buildings, biomass fuels from sun-nourished organic crops and wastes, electricity from solar cells, steam power from solar-thermal installations, power produced by wind machines, and energy generated by ocean temperature differences caused by the sun.

As you can see, *combinations* of energy forms will be far more important than the development of any single source.

THE MOST PRACTICAL AND PROMISING USES

Of all the solar technologies today, hot water and space heating are the most practical and economical. About one fourth of America's energy requirements are for these two purposes alone. Solar water heaters for the home are nothing new. In fact, they were quite popular in some of the sunnier climes of the United States, like Florida, as far back as 1920.

The idea of using the sun for heating water might have been pursued and developed into a substantial industry, one that later would have alleviated America's dependence on foreign oil. But two factors contributed to the decline. One was that the systems were crude and the water tanks poorly constructed. People lost faith in this form of energy. The other factor was the ready availability of natural gas at such a low cost (particularly in the South) that economy was by no means the same kind of incentive it is today.

Now the situation has become reversed. There are all kinds of practical and promising products on the market that are being produced by literally hundreds of different manufacturers, large and small. Would-be purchasers are cautioned, however, by solar consultants and government experts to survey the market carefully, to compare prices, and to check out the reliability of the sellers.

The following checklist is included to give an idea of practical solar energy applications. All such products, systems, and installations should be vastly improved by the early 1990s and certainly will be much less expensive than they are today.

Solar energy "packages." Complete, ready-made systems designed for prefabricated homes. They consist of roof collectors, air ducts, piping and tubing, large water storage tanks, pumps, and thermostats. "Packages" are designed for specific home models and vary greatly in price, depending upon the size of the residence and its intended location.

Auxiliary systems. Furnaces and boilers powered by conventional fuels such as oil and natural gas. These are much smaller in size than those used for primary heating and hot water, their capacities dependent upon the climate and the percentage of time they will be called into use during an average year.

Domestic hot water kits. Owners of conventionally heated homes can purchase any of several dozen different kits designed to supply up to 75 percent of the hot water supply. The kits can be installed by anyone handy with tools or by a plumbing contractor.

Solar collectors. Flat plate collectors are the most common kind, since they can be affixed to any slanting roof with a southern exposure and used for space heating and hot water. They range widely in sizes. They also vary greatly in design and the kinds of materials used, including glass, plastic, steel, aluminum, copper, and tin. Collectors may be ordered separately or with pipes and ducts.

Water storage tanks. Most of these are large—much larger than the conventional hot water tank—and range from one thousand gallons to two or three times that capacity. They must be strong to be serviceable and are always heavily insulated.

Solar fluids. Chemicals under various trade names are promoted for use in solar energy systems on the basis of their capacity to transfer

Students at the Bronx High School of Science (left) examine the solar panels used to provide hot water heating at their school. Some solar systems, such as the one at the Gainesville, Florida, airport (right), can both heat and cool buildings.

more heat more quickly than ordinary water. Some of these chemicals have been proven very effective in the laboratory, as well as in actual use.

Solar controls. Unlike conventional thermostats, controls for solar equipment operate on a kind of sliding scale. That is, they respond with more sensitivity. Instead of cutting the furnace on or off whenever the preset temperature is reached, they slow down or speed up the heat collecting process as the sun changes in intensity. Even on cloudy days there are usually enough rays slipping through so that some heat can be obtained, either for storage or direct use.

Greenhouses. Once designed solely for the growing of flowers and plants by home gardeners, greenhouses now have a secondary (sometimes primary) purpose: to assist in capturing and distributing heat. The "new breed" of greenhouse has been described as one that manufactures and stores most of the heat for its own use and has plenty left over to contribute to the house to which it is attached. This is made possible by new kinds of insulated glass and plastic, by the use of heat-retaining floors and inner walls, and by complex systems of insulated blinds that retain warmth at night and during overcast days.

Swimming pool heaters. There are two basic kinds of products for pools. One is the conventional cover, well insulated, that is pulled over the pool at night or during cold weather. The other is a modest-

sized solar collection device (sometimes portable) that circulates water and warms it in the process.

Solar stoves. These range from small, lightweight models that can be taken on camping trips, to full-sized grills and ovens that are permanently installed on patios or in other outdoor recreation areas. They consist of mirrored bowls that focus the sun's heat on a central burner or oven. They are limited to use on sunny or semisunny days, but can generate great amounts of heat quickly.

Air conditioners. Although cooling devices for the home have been available for many years, solar air conditioners are new to the field and not too practical for anything but large residences or commercial installations. Still, they will come into their own during the next decade or so.

Solar batteries. The military services have been using solar storage batteries for many years, going back to World War II, when they were important in remote outposts or for emergencies. Now they are becoming available to the public. They resemble conventional storage batteries, but have charging units that derive their power from the sun.

Solar gadgets. These range from solar-operated radios and cassette players to outdoor fans and insect killers. You can also buy a sundial with chimes, a small clothes-washing machine, an automatic water pump for garden or lawn, and a variety of games—all operated by the sun.

Solar Research Projects

RESEARCH AND DEVELOPMENT

Research in the field of solar energy has been erratic and spotty over the years. Several ambitious U.S. government projects were scrapped when federal budgets were cut. Solar energy had long been considered less vital than other energy forms and in some cases even a kind of amusing toy. That attitude began to change in the 1970s when it became evident that the world's supplies of oil and natural gas were limited and that prices for all of the conventional fuels were suddenly skyrocketing.

By the early 1980s, at least thirty states had enacted, or begun to enact, legislation to encourage the construction of solar homes and commercial buildings. Many of the laws provided tax credits for solar installations. Other laws made it possible for builders to construct solar collectors and other additions to existing structures that might not previously have been allowed under local building codes.

The ultimate effect of this change in outlook was to motivate many of the largest American corporations to commit time, money, and scientists to solar research and development (R&D) programs. Among such corporations entering the field, or enlarging their solar capabilities, were General Electric, Honeywell, ITT, Westinghouse, General Motors, Owens-Illinois, Libby-Owens-Ford, PPG, Grumman, and Dow Corning.

At the government level, the most important developer of solar energy systems has been the National Aeronautics and Space Administration (NASA). Its long-range R&D programs have created more efficient solar batteries, collectors, machinery, and instruments for satellites, manned spacecraft, and the dramatically successful space shuttle. One of the most important advances was the creation of large winglike arrays of solar cells for the shuttle to collect sunlight for the production of energy. These can generate twenty-five kilowatts of power, not only for the orbiting ship but for experiments on board.

NASA has been developing solar electric propulsion units with capacities of several hundred kilowatts. These are valuable in supplying the energy necessary to move large objects in space from low orbits to high orbits. Such power units will make it possible, too, to send spacecraft on lengthy scientific missions to the outer planets.

R&D FOR OUTER SPACE

"Energy shortages and pollution worries, and the prospect of worse to come," says a spokesman for NASA, "have focused special interest on the idea of converting space sunlight—unlimited, unfiltered by the atmosphere, uninterrupted by nightfall—into electricity for consumers on earth." The respected American Institute for Aeronautics and Astronautics (AIAA) selected this kind of space power as one of the three most promising ways "to use the unique environment of space to help solve problems that are complicated by gravity and the atmosphere."

Furthermore, reports a long-range study made by AIAA, "There is little question of technical feasibility: all elements of prospective power plants have been established by either experimental tests or long periods of operation in space. . . ."

Among the advantages listed for locating solar power plants in orbit were: isolation from populated places, no earthquake hazards, the easy disposal of excess heat, savings of natural resources by lightweight construction, no corrosion of materials, no pollution, and no need for energy storage or backup power facilities.

One of the United States government's largest research projects in the solar field was the development of solar stills for converting sea

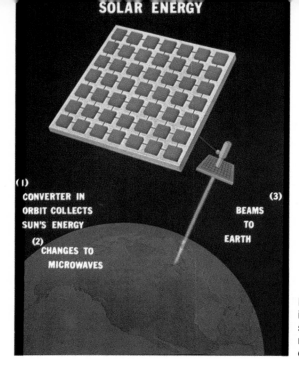

SOLAR ENERGY

(1)
CONVERTER IN
ORBIT COLLECTS
SUN'S ENERGY
(2)
CHANGES TO
MICROWAVES

(3)
BEAMS
TO
EARTH

Drawing of a solar power station in space that would collect the sun's energy, convert it into microwaves, and beam it down to earth.

water to fresh water. Population increases and larger per capita use of water prompted a widespread movement to improve our sources. Other motivating factors were escalating problems of drought, both in large cities and in agricultural regions, as well as the overwhelming water pollution problems that have been the concern of environmentalists across the nation.

Solar stills have proved to be one of the knottiest areas of research. Thus far, experimental stills have required many acres of equipment just to produce a few thousand gallons of fresh water. And costs have been so high that it has been far more economical to use oil or other conventional fuels in the heating and evaporation processes.

More and more scientific groups have undertaken solar programs and projects. The American Society of Mechanical Engineers, for example, formed a special committee on solar energy and committed many of its members to related activities. The American Institute of Architects has been researching methods of blending solar energy systems more compatibly into exterior and interior building designs. The American Society of Heating, Refrigerating, and Air Conditioning Engineers has pioneered in the technology of adapting conventionally powered equipment to solar power.

The past three decades have seen the birth of a number of trade and professional associations whose objectives are the development of solar energy. The first of importance in the United States was the Association for Applied Solar Energy, formed in the middle 1950s. Its purpose was to stimulate research for the more effective utilization of solar energy. Working with the Stanford Research Institute and the University of Arizona, AFASE sponsored the First World Symposium on Applied Solar Energy. Some nine hundred scientists, engineers, and researchers from thirty-six countries presented papers and demonstrated about ninety solar devices. These included small steam-driven engines, radios, ovens, batteries, and other inventions that were entirely solar powered.

Similar organizations that have come into being are the International Solar Energy Society (1970), which publishes three periodicals on solar energy; the Solar Energy Industries Association (1974), which supports a research and education foundation; the Solar Energy Institute of North America (1976), composed of manufacturers, architects, engineers, and educators; and the National Association of Solar Contractors (1977), which serves as a clearinghouse for technical information and represents the industry before Congress and the Department of Energy.

Today, many of the country's major universities are engaged in solar energy research. Among them are the Universities of Arizona, California, Florida, and New Mexico, Massachusetts Institute of Technology, Carnegie-Mellon University, New York University, and Penn State—just to name a very few.

RESEARCH ABROAD

Until recently, the United States was considerably behind several other nations in the matter of solar energy research. The Soviet Union has long been active in R&D, particularly in its own space program. Soviet scientists have successfully completed a number of large installations that use the sun to make steam and then generate electricity. Although exact figures are not available, it is safe to assume that the

Compound parabolic converter (left). Parabolic trough solar collector (right).

Soviets are saving millions of gallons of oil each day by using the sun to run power plants at least part of the time.

It is said that there are more solar water heaters in Japan than in the rest of the world combined. Whether this is accurate or not, it is certainly true that Japan has pioneered in developing solar energy for many practical purposes. The Japanese were early developers of small solar batteries to power certain types of electronic equipment. Food processing, long a specialized and honored art in Japan, has been implemented by the use of various kinds of solar cookers, as well as by solar methods of processing and preserving foods. The government has been sponsoring extensive solar research projects for many years, in some cases going back to the 1930s.

Israel has been engaged in solar research almost since it achieved independence in 1948, spurred on by the fact that it has plenty of sunlight and an urgent need for sources of energy. The National Physical Laboratory of Israel and the Israel Institute of Technology have undertaken large solar research programs over the years. They were so successful in the development of a solar water heater that the country's electric utilities had to drop their rates to compete with the sun-powered product. Until that time, no solar products in any country had achieved such an economic milestone.

One of the significant research projects in Israel was known as a "solar pond," developed by a solar pioneer who headed a laboratory there to study energy from the sun. His name was Harry Tabor. He recalled a childhood incident in a pond. Contrary to every other place he had swum, the water near the bottom (about six feet down) was warmer than at the top. What was it that had been different? Many years later, he came up with the answer. The water had been much denser at the bottom. Experimenting with a man-made pond three feet deep at the National Physical Laboratory, he duplicated the phenomenon. He made the water at the bottom denser by adding salt, which sank, and by lining the bottom with black plastic to absorb heat. During the heat of the day, the pond reached an incredible 200 degrees Fahrenheit at the bottom.

Over a period of time, he discovered that the pond was gradually heating the earth around it. Also, because the hot water was down below, not at the surface where it might cool or evaporate, it retained its high temperature even on cloudy days and during the night. He was able to invent a small turbine that could run on the hot water piped out of the lower layer of water. Although it was never a practical success, it revealed facts about solar heating that one day may be valuable in the quest to harness the sun.

Another country noted for its pioneering in solar energy is West Germany. Interestingly enough, some of the research experiments there have also centered around the creation of artificial solar ponds. In this case, however, the ponds were partially heated by warm waste water from nearby power plants. With temperatures increased by solar energy, the water would be circulated through buildings as a supplementary source of heat.

One of the foremost solar pioneers in Germany is Dr. Nikolaus Laing. He has invented numerous solar devices that have proven themselves. But he also has a vivid imagination. One of his favorite plans uses the intense heat of the Sahara in North Africa to turn water into steam. The steam would then be pumped rapidly under the Mediterranean Sea to Europe where it could power various types of machines and generators. Then, as the steam cooled and condensed back into hot water, it could be used to heat homes, melt ice on the roads, and perhaps irrigate year-round crops in hothouses.

Although such an ambitious plan has never been carried out, Laing was able to demonstrate quite convincingly that the heating, transportation, and storage methods he advocated could work in actual practice. In the course of testing the various components for this kind of system, Laing and his scientific associates perfected a number of other inventions and methods for applying solar energy.

Many nations have extensive solar research projects. All are not necessarily in those parts of the globe that we think of as being blessed with months of intense sunlight. Egypt, Sri Lanka (Ceylon), and India are engaged in solar research. Yet so are Canada and England, Denmark and Sweden. The Peoples' Republic of China, Australia, New Zealand, South Africa, and Switzerland also have solar projects. In fact, there is hardly a country in the world that is not trying to harness the sun and avoid the problems and expense of supplying power in increasing amounts by the old, conventional methods.

Scientists continue to experiment. The research they do in laboratories someday will bring low-cost, practical solar-powered energy systems into homes.

The chemist (below) is checking a type of solar cell that uses sunlight to produce hydrogen from water. The single crystal silicon wafer he holds is the starting material for the cell.

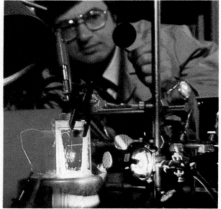

PROTECTING THE ENVIRONMENT

"The attractions of solar energy are many," said one author in a treatise advocating more reliance on the sun. "In a monetary sense, solar energy costs nothing; it is free for the taking and will not run out for billions of years. It doesn't pollute or otherwise damage the environment. It creates no dangerous waste products. . . ."

One of the basic benefits of using solar energy is that it is in total harmony with the environment, whether it is captured in the heart of a great American city or employed for agricultural uses in a remote region of a Third World nation. This truth appeals to many groups of ecologists who are deeply concerned about oil spills and acid rain and the harmful stack emissions from public utilities that burn sulfurous coal.

The important fact about solar energy is that it is a direct, natural source. It requires no combustion and, therefore, leaves no residue. "Solar will have its own environmental problems," commented one energy specialist, "but they will be minor."

In comparing solar energy with coal, oil, natural gas, and nuclear energy, one of solar's substantial long-range advantages is that it is compatible with the environment.

"It will not be the renewable aspect of solar energy but its nonpolluting nature which will make it an essential source," commented an energy consultant to the United Nations. "For it is not only air and water pollution which may cause a halt [to the growth of other fuels], but it may very well be thermal pollution, the disposal of waste heat, which will limit the use of fossil fuels and nuclear energy.

"The burning of these fuels releases their stored potential energy and converts it into heat. The solar energy which falls on the earth enters into the heat balance whether it is temporarily used by man for work or not. It is the only source of energy which does not contribute thermal pollution."

In a unique way, solar energy is an active force in protecting the environment and combating pollution. Already the U.S. government has established environmental monitoring stations across the country.

Automatic instruments register air and water pollution levels. Solar cells are being used to provide the power for these unmanned stations and for the radio transmitters that send out daily readings.

THE CONSERVATION OF ENERGY

A solar home is not merely a residence that has visible solar collectors on a slanting roof and facilities for storing heat in the basement. Rather, it is a house that has been purposely designed to be *energy conserving*. It may draw as little as 25 percent or as much as 75 percent of its energy needs from the sun, and rely on conventional fuels for the rest. Its design is important, however, for it uses all kinds of ingenious techniques, devices, and improvements to conserve heat.

Why go to so much trouble to conserve energy when the rays of the sun are free and going to waste?

The answer is that every ray of sunlight that can be captured and put to use is precious. Collecting systems are large in size, relatively inefficient, and able to function successfully for only a small percentage of the time. Conservation is vital, not to avoid using up this energy source, but to concentrate what can be obtained in an efficient and economical way.

One of the best and most graphic examples of this concept was the "Conservation Home" built by Con Edison in Briarcliff Manor, New York, and displayed to the public in the early 1980s. It was one of several energy conservation projects undertaken by the company.

The house contained 2,360 square feet of living space, which included four bedrooms, two-and-a-half bathrooms, a living room, dining room, family room, kitchen, greenhouse, and atrium. It also had a large deck, porch, and two-car garage.

In appearance, it was designed to be comparable to other homes in the community—with one major exception. It required less than half as much heating fuel as a conventionally built home of similar size. The house was built with walls specially designed to retain heat in

M.I.T.'s solar building number 5 (top left), its interior (above left), and its pavilion (right)

cold weather and keep the interior cooler during hot summer days. Thermal windows were also featured, as well as passive solar materials to assist with space heating and an active solar system to heat water. Other solar features included:

• A greenhouse, atrium, and numerous windows and skylights on the south side to catch the sun's light and heat. Movable insulating shades in the greenhouse and atrium prevented heat loss at night and on cloudy days.

• A minimum number of windows on the cold north side.

• Two collector panels on the south slope of the roof for the solar water system.

• Buffer zones separating the living room from the outside air. The use of a vestibule made it possible to close the outside door before the inner one was opened.

• All windows positioned in such a way that they would catch the winter sun, but be shaded in the summer when the angle of the sun was higher.

• Tile-covered concrete floors in the living room and family room,

Two views of an underground solar home

to absorb the sun's heat in winter and release it slowly to warm the interior.

• A vent near the top of the atrium to draw off solar-heated air as it rises and mixes with the air in the furnace.

• A three-part "zone" arrangement, each with its own thermostat, so that heat is delivered only where and when it is needed.

• A "heat exchanger" ventilation system. This makes it possible for a home to be properly ventilated with a minimal loss of heat, since much of the heat that would otherwise escape is recycled.

• Solar water heating to provide all the hot water needed in the summer and about half of the average requirements for other seasons.

SUBTERRANEAN LIVING

The ultimate example of conservation is probably the house that is built underground. There are a surprising number of them in the United States. Since most people cringe at the idea of living like moles, a compromise solution is the house that is only partially underground, with a full south facade. The north, east, and west walls are partially banked with earth and depend for light on a few upper windows and skylights.

10 Our Solar Future

CONCLUSION

How soon will we really live in a solar world, one where the sun is dominant and everything on earth relies on it? In point of fact, the earth was truly a solar world millions of years ago before human beings evolved and eventually discovered how to make fire. Oil and natural gas and uranium and coal all existed in prehistoric times. But they lay dormant, while the sun provided the only source of energy for plant and animal life.

From a practical standpoint, we will see a Solar Age, according to many energy experts, shortly after we enter the twenty-first century. Yet it will be such in name only, for we will rely on nuclear energy and today's conventional fuels for a good many commonplace energy purposes. It is doubtful, for example, that solar energy will play a predominant part in transportation, except for use in space vehicles beyond the earth's atmosphere.

Solar energy will also be at a great disadvantage in extremely northern and southern climes where the winter months are locked in almost perpetual darkness. Energy from the sun probably will, of course, be transported in the future almost anywhere in storage batteries or power lines. But there are limits as to the practicality of doing so when fuel oil or nuclear energy could supply all of the energy needs right on site.

In summation, solar energy offers the following positive advantages over one or more of the other forms of energy that have been available during the twentieth century:

- *Safety*. It will not burn, explode, cause harmful side effects to people through radiation, or pose any mechanical dangers. It requires few moving parts, except for the flow of air and water. When concentrated to provide heat in an intensity that could cause burns or fire, it is always confined in a manner that permits very little chance of accident. Although solar energy can be converted to electricity, which can electrocute victims or cause fires, the electricity is no more prevalent than might be generated by other fuels.

- *Clean environment*. Air pollution and water pollution are nonexistent in solar energy systems. The sun, in fact, is being used actively to help monitor and clean up the environment.

- *Universality*. There is no nation on earth that is without sunlight. Even those in cold climates or plagued with more than their share of rain and clouds have access to a million times the amount of solar energy they could ever consume. This is in direct contrast to coal, oil, natural gas, and uranium, which are commercially available in relatively few locations.

- *Limitless resources*. The energy that reaches the earth from the sun will not diminish for millions upon millions of years. Fossil fuels, to the contrary, are rapidly being depleted. In addition, they become harder and harder to locate and more and more costly to produce.

- *Lessening costs*. Although solar power is expensive today, its cost-per-kilowatt will continue to decrease steadily. The cost of installations will drop dramatically as the basic units and items of related equipment are mass-produced on a highly competitive basis.

A LOOK AT THE SOLAR FUTURE

Of all the predictions for the future of solar energy installations, none is more exciting than the concept of the satellite power station orbiting the earth. Such a station would be constantly bathed in the strongest sunlight and its power could be beamed as readily to the remotest locations on earth as to the world's great cities.

Many scientists have been working, both individually and in teams, on one or more aspects of the power satellite. Arthur D. Little, Inc., a

The solar cell array would be used to supply energy to supply bases of the future. This sketch shows living facilities for ten workers, plus work areas.

research and development firm near Boston, has already prepared detailed plans for an experimental model referred to as SSPS (Solar Satellite Power Station). The station would, in fact, be two units orbiting some eight thousand miles from each other. The reason for the twin satellites is to prevent any interruption in the generation of power when the earth's shadow temporarily obscures the sun from a single unit.

There are many designs possible for a power station in space. Each, however, incorporates the wings shown in photographs of small spacecraft, which are in reality panels made up of thousands of solar cells. The wings, or panels, of the power station would be many times larger, covering an area of perhaps ten square miles. Since there is no wind in outer space, they could not be blown off or bent. The only problem might be bombardment by small bits of matter floating through space, which would destroy individual cells on contact.

As the cells absorb energy from the sun, they would generate electricity. The electricity would then be beamed from a transmitting antenna to a huge receiving antenna on earth. A solar satellite power station of this experimental size (considered very moderate in capacity) could transmit enough electricity to supply a medium-sized city.

Solar cells power this experimental irrigation project near Mead, Nebraska. Solar power converted into electricity is used to pump water to eighty acres of corn and soybeans.

SOLAR FARMS

Another concept for the future is the *solar farm,* ideally located in a desert region where the sun shines brightly almost every day of the year. The farms would actually "harvest" sunshine, using flat plate collectors to absorb immense amounts of heat. The heat would be used to turn water into steam to run turbines and generate electricity. Another method would be to use solar cells and batteries, generating electricity directly.

In either case, the electricity could be transmitted many miles through power lines, just as has been done for many years from conventional power plants. One of the attractive aspects of any solar farm is that inhabitants of nearby communities would not have to worry about harmful radiation, air pollution, or wastes running off into streams.

Solar farms of this kind would require an area of about one square mile to supply the power needs of approximately fifteen thousand homes.

These are but a few of the ideas, proposals, and experiments that establish solar energy as a practical and promising way to meet the increasing power and fuel needs of the future.

Aerial view of Sandia National Laboratories in Albuquerque, New Mexico

GLOSSARY

The following words and phrases are but a few of those that are being used to describe some of the installations, theories, products, techniques, and activities in the field of solar energy.

active solar energy system. One that uses mechanical methods and an outside source of energy to operate the system.

ampere. A unit of electrical current used to denote the amount of power flowing through a circuit.

array. A bank of solar-collecting devices hooked together to increase their capacity.

atrium. A closed interior court into which other rooms open. It is often used in a passive solar energy system to supply air used to warm other areas.

auxiliary power. Power produced by conventional fuels, such as oil or gas, to supplement a solar energy system.

backup energy system. The same as "auxiliary power." It is most often used at night or when days are overcast.

biomass. Materials derived from organic sources, essentially waste materials that are burned to produce energy.

boiler. The name for what we often call a furnace. A large, strong container in which water can be turned to steam for heating, or for producing electricity.

British thermal unit (Btu). The amount of heat required to raise the temperature of one pound of water one degree Fahrenheit. The Btu is the standard unit of measurement for all forms of heat and energy.

collector. Any device that collects heat from the sun and transmits it to another location.

concentrating collector. One that uses mirrors, lenses, or other devices to focus the sun's radiation more intensely on a smaller surface.

condensation. The process of changing a vapor into a liquid through cooling.

conduction. The flow of heat between a hot material and a colder material when both are in direct contact.

convection. The transfer of heat by the flow of air or water, as from a roof collector to a storage tank below.

cooling pond. A body of water that loses heat from its surface by evaporation, convection, or radiation.

degree day. A unit of measurement for defining a fixed temperature (usually 65 degrees Fahrenheit) and the average temperature for the day.

diffused. Scattered; often said of the sun's radiation, which is often weak and indirect.

double-glazed. Covered by two layers of glass or clear plastic. Used in describing insulated or storm windows and doors. (Triple-glazing is sometimes used for windows on the coldest sides of a building.)

efficiency of conversion. The relationship between the actual amount of energy derived from a source and the total energy available. Usually expressed as a percentage.

flat plate collector. A solar-collecting unit in which the energy from the sun is converted into heat on a flat surface containing coils that carry air or liquid.

fossil fuels. Organic compounds formed by the decay of matter under heat and pressure millions of years ago. Coal, oil, natural gas, and peat fall into this category.

Glauber's salt. Sodium sulfate (named after the chemist who discovered it). Since it melts at a mere 90 degrees Fahrenheit and changes rapidly from liquid to solid and back, it can be used to store heat more effectively than water or many other solids and liquids.

greenhouse. In passive solar design, an attached windowed area from which heat is drawn to help warm the interior of the adjacent building. (It may or may not be used for plants.)

greenhouse effect. A phenomenon whereby rays of the sun enter a glassed area and warm floors and walls. Because the wave length changes upon striking the inside, the rays cannot escape and are useful in providing warmth.

heat exchanger. A device that transfers heat from one fluid or medium to another.

heat pipe. A closed pipe from which the air has been removed and replaced by a liquid that is alternately liquefied and vaporized to intensify the heat.

heat pump. A device that both heats and cools, employing mechanical and chemical action in the process. When cooling, the pump functions much like an air conditioner, removing unwanted heat from the source.

heliostat. A device with a mirror mounted on an axis in such a way that it can be rotated to reflect the sun in a certain direction.

hydrocarbon. Any compound containing only hydrogen and carbon, such as crude oil or coal.

hydroelectricity. Electric power that is produced from the energy of water flowing downstream or falling from a height, as over a dam.

insolation. The amount of solar radiation striking a surface exposed to the sky over a certain period of time.

insulation. A material that increases the resistance to the flow of heat.

kilowatt. A unit of power equal to one thousand watts.

kilowatt hour. The amount of energy equivalent to one kilowatt of power being used for one hour.

langley. A measure of solar radiation. It equals one calorie of heat per square centimeter, or 3.69 Btus per square foot.

megawatt. Unit of power equal to one million watts.

nonrenewable energy source. A mineral energy source that is in limited supply, such as gas, oil, coal, and nuclear fuels.

passive energy system. One in which heat is gathered through direct, nonmechanical means, such as through windows facing south or the accumulaton of heat (or cold) in a thick wall.

photoelectric cell. A device that produces electric current when sunlight or other light shines upon it.

photovoltaic cell. Similar to a "photoelectric cell."

radiant energy. See "solar energy."

radiation. The means by which energy flows from one body to another when the bodies are separated by a space, even in a vacuum.

renewable energy source. Certain forms of energy that are not consumed or limited, such as solar energy and other sources derived from it, including wind, hydroelectricity, and biomass.

rock bin. A heat storage container filled with rocks or pebbles, used in solar heating and cooling systems.

silicon cells. Photovoltaic generators whose base material is silicon, one of the earth's most abundant resources.

solar cell. One that uses sunlight as a light source. See "photoelectric cell."

solar collector. See "collector."

solar cooker. A device used to focus the sun's rays for the purpose of cooking food.

solar electricity. Electricity generated directly from sunlight.

solar energy. Radiant energy produced by the sunlight that reaches the earth or its outer atmosphere.

solar farm. A large area of land upon which arrays of solar collectors have been set up to harvest solar energy for practical use.

solar furnace. A device, usually using large mirrors, to focus and intensify the heat of the sun at a certain point.

solarium. A living space enclosed by glass or clear plastic. Similar to a greenhouse.

solar power. The rate at which solar energy is produced, usually measured in kilowatt hours.

solar radiation. Energy radiated from the sun.

solar satellite power station. A giant solar energy collecting platform in orbit around the earth.

solar still. A device that distills fresh water from sea water by evaporation and heat from the sun.

solar-thermal conversion. Any method using the sun's heat to drive turbines and produce electricity.

solar water heater. An installation that supplies hot water by using the heat from the sun.

thermal mass. The heat capacity of a building material, such as brick, adobe, or concrete.

tracking. Using mechanical or other means so that a thermal device, such as a collector, can tilt to follow the sun.

Trombe wall. Thick masonry blackened and exposed to the sun behind glass in order to store and distribute heat.

turbine. An engine driven by the pressure of steam, air, or water against curved vanes. One step in the generation of electricity.

zoned heating. The control of temperature in a room, or rooms, independent of other areas in the same building.

BIBLIOGRAPHY

Adam, F. *Catch a Sunbeam: A Book of Solar Study and Experiments*. New York. Hartcourt Brace Jovanovich, 1978.

Barling, John. *Solar Fun Book: Eighteen Projects for the Weekend Builder*. Andover, MA. Brick House Publishing Co., 1979.

Clark, Wilson. *Energy for Survival*. New York. Anchor Press/Doubleday, 1975.

Crowther, Richard. *Sun-Earth*. New York. Scribner's, 1978.

Diamond, Stuart, and Lorris, Paul. *It's In Your Power*. New York. Rawson Associates, 1978.

Hayes, D. *Energy: The Solar Prospect*. Washington, DC. Worldwatch Institute, 1977.

Hoke, J. *Solar Energy*. New York. Franklin Watts, 1978.

Knight, David. *Harnessing the Sun: The Story of Solar Energy*. New York. Morrow, 1976.

Kraft, B.H. *Careers in the Energy Industry*. New York. Franklin Watts, 1977.

Lyons, Steve (ed.). *Sun: A Handbook for the Solar Decade*. San Francisco. Friends of the Earth, 1978.

Spetgang, Tilly, and Wells, Malcolm. *The Children's Solar Energy Book*. New York. Sterling, 1982.

U.S. government, Superintendent of Documents, U.S. Government Printing Office, Washington, DC 20402:

   In the Bank or Up the Chimney (Stock #023-000-00297-3), 1983. $1.70

Also available, at no cost are *various short publications on solar energy*. Write: Solar Heating, P.O. Box 1607, Rockville, MD 20850.

INDEX

Abbot, Charles Greeley, 46
absorber, air-conditioner, 58
absorption cooler, 57
active solar energy systems, 36, 37, 59, 85
adobe dwellings, 6
Aerospace Corporation, 19
air conditioning, solar, 51, 57, 58, 75
aircraft, solar-powered, 55
Algeria, 6
Allen, Edward, 50
alternate energy systems, 68–71
American Institute for Aeronautics and Astronautics (AIAA), 77
American Institute of Architects, 78
American Petroleum Institute, 51
American Society of Heating, Refrigerating, and Air Conditioning Engineers, 78
American Society of Mechanical Engineers, 78
Archimedes, 5
architects, 65
Arizona, 9, 19, 23
Arsonval, Jacques d', 27
Arthur D. Little, Inc., 88
Association of Applied Solar Energy, 46, 79
associations, 79
Atacama Desert, Chile, 45
Atlanta, Georgia, 53
atmosphere, and the sun, 13, 21
Audubon Society, 54
Australia, 10, 16, 17, 82
automobiles, sun-powered, 54, 55
auxiliary solar energy systems, 72
bags, plastic, solar collector, 33, 34, 35
Baker electric car, 54
batteries, solar-powered, 19, 29, 51, 75, 80, 90
Bell Telephone Laboratories, 39, 46
biomass, 70
Briarcliff Manor, New York, 84
bridges, anti-corrosion devices, 52
British thermal units (Btus), 14
Business Week magazine, 62
California, 11, 22, 34, 53, 69
California State Polytechnic College, 33
Canada, 82
careers, solar energy field, 64, 65
Carnegie-Mellon University, 79

Caus, Salomon de, 44
cells, solar, 17, 18, 24–26, 38–42, 51, 52, 55, 77, 84, 89, 90
Ceylon, 82
Chile, 45
China, 82
closed-loop system, 47
coal, 7, 9, 10, 12, 13, 43, 56, 68, 70, 71, 83
collectors, solar, 11, 28–37, 46, 47, 49, 57, 61, 73
collectors, solar, concentrating, 30, 31, 53
collectors, solar, evacuated tube, 35
Colorado, 6, 54
computer programmers and operators, 65
concentrating collectors, 30, 31, 53
condenser, air-conditioner, 58
"Conservation Home," 84
conservation of energy, 84–86
Consolidated Edison Company, 47, 48, 84
controls, solar, 74
conversion, direct, 37
conversion, indirect, 37
cookers (stoves), solar, 19, 30, 38, 46, 75, 80
cooling, solar, 51, 55–57
cost, solar systems, 66–68, 88
Denmark, 82
Denver Community College, 54
devices and equipment, solar, 18, 19, 38–43, 47–52, 63, 64, 72–75
diffuseness, of solar energy, 28
direct conversion, 37
domestic hot water heater kits, 73
Dow Corning, 76
early uses of solar energy, 5–11, 44–46
Eastern Sun Power Company, 10
ecology stations, 44
economics, of solar power, 66
Egypt, 6, 8, 9, 10, 82
electricity, solar-generated, 10, 15, 16, 18, 22, 24, 27, 35, 39–42, 51, 55, 61, 66, 77, 89, 90
Electric Power Research Institute, 66
Eneas, A.G., 9
energy, conserving, 84–86
Energy Research and Development Administration (ERDA), 71
engines, solar-powered, 8, 9, 40, 46

England, 82
English Channel, 55
environment, and solar energy, 43, 44, 83, 88
equipment and devices, solar, 18, 19, 38–43, 47–52, 63, 64, 72–75
Ericsson, John, 8
evacuated tube collectors, 35
evaporator, air-conditioner, 58
evaporators, 19
farming, and solar energy, 52
farms, solar, 90
First World Symposium on Applied Solar Energy, 79
flat plate solar collectors, 31–33, 37, 73, 90
Florida, 10, 27, 72
fluids, solar, 73
France, 8, 10, 16, 38, 44, 45, 46
fuels, synthetic, 70, 71
furnaces, solar, 8, 38, 45
future of solar energy, 87–90
gadgets, solar, 75
General Electric, 76
General Motors, 76
generator, air-conditioner, 58
geography, and solar energy, 20–23
Georgia, 42, 53
Georgia Power Company, 53
geothermal energy, 69
Germany, 45, 81
Geysers Geothermal Field, California, 69
Glauber's salt (sodium sulfate), 60, 61
government representatives, 65
Greece, 5, 8
"greenhouse effect," 51
greenhouses, 7, 35, 50, 74, 85
ground cooling, 56
Grumman, 76
Gulf of Mexico, 52
heat exchanger, 48, 86
heating, solar, 48–51, 59, 63, 64, 66, 67
heat pipes, solar, 63, 64
heat pumps, 62, 63
heliostats, 31
highway safety systems, 42, 43, 52
history of solar energy, 5–11
homes, solar, 6, 7, 11, 33, 47–51, 66, 67, 84–86
Honeywell, 19, 76
hot-water heaters, solar, 10, 17, 19, 30, 47–49, 72, 73, 80
hydroelectric power, 15, 37
India, 82
Indians, American, 6

indirect conversion, 37
infrared rays, of sun, 51
insolation, solar, 20
International Solar Energy Society, 79
inventors, solar devices, 8–10, 44–46
Israel, 10, 16, 17, 80, 81
Israel Institute of Technology, 80
ITT, 76
Japan, 10, 17, 80
jobs, solar energy field, 64, 65
kilns, 19
kilowatt, 15
kilowatt hour, 15
Kircher, Athanasius, 45
Laing, Nikolaus, 81, 82
Langley, Samuel, 20
langley (solar-radiation measure), 20
Las Salinas, Chile, 45
Lavoisier, Antoine, 8, 45
Libby-Owens-Ford, 76
Libya, 6
light shelves, 36
Lincoln, Massachusetts, 54
map, solar, 22
Massachusetts, 54
Massachusetts Institute of Technology (M.I.T.), 11, 50, 61, 79
mechanical power, from the sun, 8, 9
Merrimac (ship), 8
Mesa Verde, Colorado, 6
meteorological observation stations, 51
Michigan, 54
Milbrook, New York, 54
mirrors, and solar energy, 8, 9, 26, 29, 30, 31, 33, 34, 35, 38, 45
Mojave Desert, 34
Monitor (ship), 8
Mont-Louis, France, 38
National Aeronautics and Space Administration (NASA), 24, 46, 76, 77
National Association of Solar Contractors, 79
National Physical Laboratory of Israel, 80, 81
National Safety Council, 42
National Science Foundation, 54
natural gas, 12, 13, 51, 56, 68–71, 72, 76, 83
navigational aids, 19, 43
New Guinea, 42
New Hampshire, 54
New Mexico, 23
New York Botanical Garden, 54
New York City, 47

New York State, 47, 54, 84
New York University, 79
New Zealand, 82
night sky radiation, 56
North Africa, 6
nuclear power, 43, 68, 69, 83
oceans, energy from, 27
Ocean Thermal Energy Conversion
    (OTEC), 27
oil (*See* petroleum)
oil shale, 71
outer space, and solar energy, 18,
    23–26, 40, 77, 88, 89
Owens-Illinois, 76
"packages," solar energy, 72
parabolic solar collectors, 31, 33
Paris, France, 46
passive solar cooling, 56
passive solar energy systems, 35,
    36, 59, 66, 85
Penn State University, 79
Pennsylvania, 10, 54
petroleum, 7, 10, 12, 13, 43, 51,
    56, 68–71, 72, 76, 83
petroleum industry, and solar
    energy, 52
Phoenix, Arizona, 9
photography, and solar energy, 38,
    39
photons, 40
photosynthesis, 16
photovoltaic cell, 38
Pifre, Able, 46
pioneers, solar inventions, 8–10,
    44–46
Pittsburgh, Pennsylvania, 54
plants, and the sun, 13, 16
pollution, 43, 44, 83, 88
ponds, solar, 34, 81
"Power Tower," 34, 35
PPG, 76
radiation, from the sun, 14, 15, 21
railroad-crossing signals, 42
Rankine Cycle solar air con-
    ditioner, 58
research and development, 76–82
reservoirs, solar, 61
Romans, 5
roof sprayers, 36
Russia, 10, 16, 79
safety, of solar energy, 88
Sahara, 81
salespersons, 65
Santa Clara, California, 53
satellites, space, 23–25, 40, 88, 89
sea, energy from, 27
shale, 71
short wave-length rays, of sun, 51
Shuman, Frank, 10
silicon, 40, 41

Skylab, 24
Sky-Therm (solar home), 33
Smithsonian Institution, 46
sodium sulfate (Glauber's salt), 60,
    61
solar air conditioning, 51, 57, 58,
    75
solar cells, 17, 18, 24–26, 38–42,
    51, 52, 55, 77, 84, 89, 90
Solar Challenger (aircraft), 55
solar collectors, 11, 28–37, 46,
    47, 49, 57, 61, 73
solar controls, 74
solar cooling, 51, 55–57
solar devices and equipment, 18,
    19, 38–43, 47–52, 63, 64,
    72–75
solar energy:
    air conditioning, 51, 57, 58, 75
    alternate energy systems, 68–71
    cooling, 51, 55–57
    cost, solar systems, 66–68, 88
    early uses, 5–11, 44–46
    energy, conserving, 84–86
    environment, 43, 44, 83, 88
    future of solar energy, 87–90
    geography, and solar energy,
        20–23
    homes, solar, 6, 7, 11, 33, 47–
        51, 66, 67, 84–86
    inventors, solar devices, 8–10,
        44–46
    jobs, solar energy field, 64, 65
    pioneers, solar inventions, 8–10,
        44–46
    research and development,
        76–82
    sea, energy from, 27
    solar cells, 17, 18, 24–26, 38–
        42, 51, 52, 55, 77, 84, 89, 90
    solar collectors, 11, 28–37, 46,
        47, 49, 57, 61, 73
    solar devices and equipment,
        types of, 18, 19, 38–43, 47–
        52, 63, 64, 72–75
    solar storage systems, 19, 29,
        59–64, 73
    spacecraft, 18, 23–26, 40, 77,
        88, 89
    sun, as energy source, 12–19,
        21, 28–30
    transportation, 54, 55
    water heaters, 10, 17, 19, 30,
        47–49, 72, 73, 80
    weather, and solar energy,
        21–23
Solar Energy Industries Associa-
    tion, 79
Solar Energy Institute of North
    America, 79

solar energy "packages," 72
solar engineers, 64
solar equipment technologists, 65
solar farms, 90
solar fluids, 73
solar furnaces, 8, 38, 45
solar gadgets, 75
solar heating, 48–51, 59, 63, 64, 66, 67
solar-heating consultants, 65
solar heat pipes, 63, 64
solar homes, 6, 7, 11, 33, 47–51, 66, 67, 84–86
solar insolation, 20
solar loop, 47, 48
solar map, 22
solar ponds, 34, 81
solar power, 15, 16, 28
solar reservoirs, 61
Solar Satellite Power Station (SSPS), 89
solar scientists, 64
solar stills, 19, 45, 46, 77, 78
solar storage systems, 19, 29, 59–64, 73
solar stoves (cookers), 19, 30, 38, 46, 74, 80
solar technicians, 64
solar-thermal conversion, 18
solar walls, 36
solar water heaters, 10, 17, 19, 30, 47–49, 72, 73, 80
South Africa, 10, 16, 82
Soviet Union (See Russia)
spacecraft, and solar energy, 18, 23–26, 40, 77, 88, 89
Stanford Research Institute, 79
stills, solar, 19, 45, 46, 77, 78
storage systems, solar, 19, 29, 59–64, 73
stoves (cookers), solar, 19, 30, 38, 46, 75, 80
sun, as energy source, 12–19, 21, 28–30
Sun Journal, The, 46
sunshine, intermittent, 28
"Sunshine Project, The," 17

Sweden, 82
swimming pool heaters, 74
Switzerland, 82
synthetic fuels, 70, 71
Tabor, Harry, 81
Tacony, Pennsylvania, 10
tar sands, 71
Tashkent, Russia, 16
telephone systems, 42
Telkes, Maria, 46
Texas, 23
thick wall construction, 56
Thomason, Harry F., 49
"tracking" the sun, 30
transportation, 54, 55
Trombe wall, 36
turbines, solar-powered, 18, 35, 58
underground houses, 86
United States Coast Guard, 43
United States Department of Energy, 54, 66, 79
United States of America, 6, 7, 9–11, 16–19, 21–24, 27, 33, 34, 42, 43, 46, 47, 49, 52–54, 61, 66, 69–72, 76–79, 83–86
United Nations, 83
University of Arizona, 19, 79
University of California, 79
University of Florida, 79
University of New Mexico, 79
Utah, 71
Vanguard I satellite, 24
walls, solar, 36
Washington, D.C., 46, 49
water heaters, solar, 10, 17, 19, 30, 47–49, 72, 73, 80
water storage tanks, 73
weather, and solar energy, 21–23
Westinghouse, 19, 76
Wilson, Charles, 45, 46
wind, cause of, 22
windmills, 15, 22
windows, and solar energy, 50, 85
World Exposition, Paris, 46
Yellowstone Park, 69
"zone" heating, 86

PICTURE ACKNOWLEDGMENTS

Black Star—© 1981 James Nachtwey, 2, 31, 74 (left), 86 (2 photos), 91
    © 1980 Kenneth Rogers, 55 (2 photos)
    © 1981 James Sugar, Aviation Advances, 74 (right)

Massachusetts Institute of Technology (M.I.T.)—50, 85 (3 photos)

Phillis Adler—11 (left), 22, 29, 34, 48

Historical Pictures Service, Chicago—4, 9, 44, 45

Department of Energy—32 (photo by Jack Schneider), 39, 69 (left),
    69 (right, Combustion Engineering, Inc.), 90

General Electric Research and Development Center—37

Sandia National Laboratories—33, 80 (right)

Argonne National Laboratory—60, 80 (left)

James P. Rowan—7 (2 photos), 58, 75 (right)

NASA—15 (right), 17, 23, 25, 26, 89

Association of American Railroads—43 (right)

American Petroleum Institute—52, 73 (left), 78

State of Wisconsin, Department of Transportation—43 (left)

National Research Council, Canada—15 (left)

Courtesy of Bell Labs—18 (left), 40 (2 photos)

Exxon Enterprises, Inc.—11 (right), 18 (middle), 73 (right), 75 (left)

Standard Oil of Indiana—67 (right), 82 (right)

Standard Oil of California—18 (right)

Olympic Resource Management—67 (left), 70 (left)

Phillips Petroleum Co.—70 (right)

Occidental Petroleum—82 (left)

E.I. du Pont de Nemours & Co.—63

Allan Roberts—13

About the Author

Wilbur Cross, a professional writer and editor, is the author of some 20 non-fiction books and several hundred magazine articles. His subjects range widely from travel and foreign culture to history, sociology, medicine, business, adventure, biography, humor, education and politics.

Mr. Cross served as a captain in the United States Army, with long service in the Pacific; worked for several years as a copywriter with a New York City advertising agency; and was an associate editor at *Life* magazine. He founded and directed his own firm, Books for Business, as an editorial director and consultant, and has worked as an editor and writer in the energy field.

Among his books are *Naval Battles and Heroes*, *Challengers of the Deep*, *Ghost Ship of the Pole*, *White House Weddings*, *Your Career in the Age of Automation*, *A Guide to Unusual Vacations*, *Kids and Booze*, and *Presidential Courage*.

For Childrens Press, Mr. Cross has written *Egypt* (Enchantment of the world series) and three **books**, *Petroleum*, *Coal*, and *Solar Energy* (Science and Technology series).

Married and the father of four daughters, he lives in Westchester County, New York.

Solar energy
Cross, Wilbur

12074

333.79 Cro

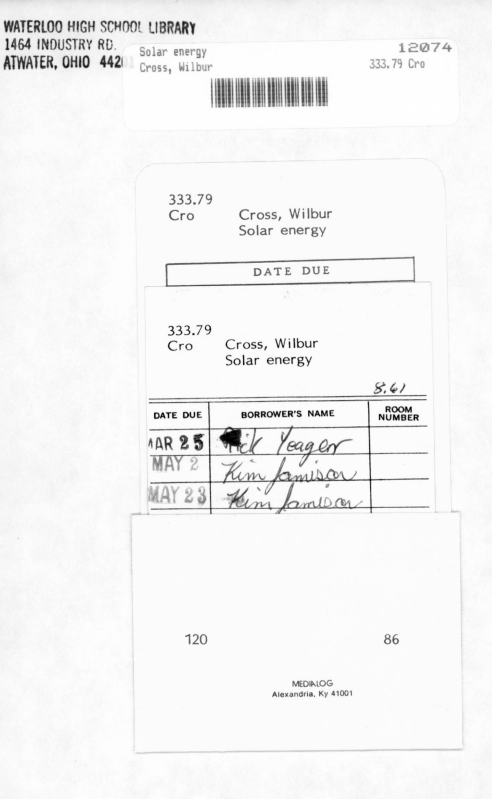

333.79
Cro   Cross, Wilbur
           Solar energy

DATE DUE

333.79
Cro   Cross, Wilbur
           Solar energy

8.61

DATE DUE	BORROWER'S NAME	ROOM NUMBER
MAR 25	Rick Yeager	
MAY 2	Kim Jamison	
MAY 23	Kim Jamison	

120   86

MEDIALOG
Alexandria, Ky 41001